Entering Light

Chris Vuille, Ph.D.

Contents

Chapter 1

Introduction

1.1 Motivations

I wrote this book because of a single moment. In that moment I came to a spontaneous and new understanding of the nature of consciousness. The event in question didn't occur during some special meditative or spiritual practice; it came while I was driving a car. The understanding was not intellectual, something I reasoned out or thought. What I observed was the same world we all live in every day, but in a totally different way. It was not subtle, it was stunning, a new mode of perception. For a moment I lost the chains of memory and imagination and perceived myself and the world as they truly are: an undivided whole.

I felt as if I'd found the keys to the universe, keys that had been in my back pocket all along. By the time I arrived at work and parked my car I resolved to write this book for my children, so if I died before they grew up they would have a guide to follow that might help them make the same discovery. In this way, I share with you my personal experience in the hope that you will also uncover the same truth, or otherwise better your life in some way.

The descriptions I will offer you are only faint echos of the actual experiences, like thinking about burning your finger as opposed to touching a hot stove. Such second-hand knowledge is important, however, because becoming aware of the possibility of change is the first step towards realizing it. I will describe the mystic experiences of the east and west, divorced from their religious and cultural settings. Together we'll try to understand the root causes of unhappiness and the nature of love, which depend on an understanding of the nature of consciousness. Seeking this understanding is the most important endeavor in anyone's life. It lies dormant within each one of us, waiting to be awakened.

1.2   Qualifications

Understanding of the kind suggested here may sound daunting to many of you. It's normal and healthy to doubt your ability to undertake such a quest. First and foremost, as you read my book, you might wonder about my own background, about whether or not I've got the right kind of experience, the ability to give you sound advice and reveal profound knowledge.

Let me assure you I'm an ordinary person just like you are. Like you, I am flawed, a work in progress. I have the same needs and desires, the same hopes and fears. My ordinariness is important; it means that anything I may have understood, you can also understand. All I can do for you is share with you my experience and point out what I understand as best I can. After that, whether you believe me or not really doesn't make any difference. Truth has nothing to do with belief: it's a matter of direct perception. Either you see it, or you don't. Further, truth isn't knowledge in the ordinary sense, like a golden rule or a mathematical equation. Truth is here and now, in the moment. In the next moment, it's only a memory.

Naturally I have had an education and have developed professional skills of various kinds. I'm a physicist. I teach at a university, write physics texts, and conduct research in relativity and quantum theory. Becoming a physicist required many years of hard study. While difficult for the uninitiated to understand, physics isn't a discipline that would necessarily lead to any self-knowledge. The only advantage such a scientific background conveys is a certain respect for the pursuit of truth and for the exact description of observed phenomena. Otherwise, my being a physicist has little to do with what I'm going to present in this book, other than perhaps help me describe accurately some extraordinary experiences.

I have only two relevant credentials. First, I'm a human being. Second, I have always had a passion for understanding not just nature, but my own nature. Now, anyone reading this book most likely has the first qualification. The second qualification is more rare. Some of us lack the passion to persist in such a difficult quest. It's easier to give up, to suppose that only very special people can uncover truth, or to simply believe what we have read or what others tell us. By the time you finish this book, however, I hope you will be persuaded that you *are* special in ways you never realized. The doors of perception can open for anyone at any time. Anyone who has consciousness can realize its nature. And even if you should go decades with only a minor glimmer of understanding, you will vastly improve your sense of well-being, your health, and your ability to cope with life's many challenges.

So if you are an ordinary human being and you have some passion for discovery, then you are qualified for the quest. And because the quest has no real ending, you can't fail. If you search with your mind and heart to better understand nature and your own nature, you will also inevitably uncover a better life.

1.3 A Brief Autobiography

In this section I sketch my life history with a few broad brushstrokes, as it relates to our spiritual quest. In reading it you'll understand that my own quest has required considerable patience and perseverance, and that it is ongoing. You'll also learn that for some decades I was oblivious to truth, struggling to understand, failing again and again. The foundation of understanding is failure. Realizing you have failed and that you're lost is the first step to finding your way.

1.3.1 Kindergarten Playground: The Quest Begins

My quest began in October of 1956 on the kindergarten playground at Shorecrest School in St.Petersburg, Florida. The campus at that time was located in the old Bayboro area, a couple blocks from Tampa Bay and Albert Whitted Airport, and consisted of old barracks painted a very light shade of aqua-green. Broken white shells carpeted the playgrounds and areas between buildings. I was a quiet and shy child, and during recess I walked alone around the playground looking at the sky and trees, at the children playing, taking it all in, as I usually did. It was a beautiful day, the grip of summer finally broken but with the sun still warm and bright. I remember looking up at the white fluffy clouds hanging in the blue sky when the following question came to me: "Where am I?"

That question may not seem very profound, but it bothered me. Where am I? What is this place and how did I end up here? These questions stayed with me several days until I came to the conclusion that I was inside my head, peering out the windows of my eyes. I liked that answer because it seemed obviously true. I felt the relief and satisfaction that comes with solving a difficult puzzle, and put the question aside. Problem solved.

The very next day my equanimity vanished. Sitting in the bedroom I shared with one of my brothers, I realized that it was very dark inside my head. If I was in there, where exactly was I?

I asked my parents where I was, and they independently gave the same answer: "You're right here". When I asked them who I was, they answered, "You're you, of course." And because the answers seemed obvious to them and incomprehensible to me, I developed the curious notion that adults understood such matters naturally, and that I would just have to wait until I was grown up in order to understand the answers for myself.

1.3.2 The Christian Years

The years passed. I didn't forget my questions, and as I grew up I kept an eye out for answers. When I was seven a little girl named Gail began luring me into the bushes so she could kiss me on the cheek. Her mother ran a Good News Club, which is a children's club for studying Christianity. I didn't realize that: I asked her if there would be any good science news, and she assured me there would be. So soon I was attending the club every week, learning about a certain form of Protestant Christianity and wondering when the science was going to start.

Following the teachings of Good News Club, I began praying to God every night, thanking him for saving me from destruction and hell, and praying for the protection of my family. I had that uncritical faith of a child which is often praised, although perhaps wrongly. I still found church and the club a little boring at times, but subscribed to the world order as it was explained to me. Down deep, however, I wasn't sure I understood what it was all about or why it should work. It was apparently another one of those mysteries that only an adult could understand.

At age eleven I experienced a crisis of faith, a moment of truth, a choice of two paths, and the consequences were very nearly as far-reaching as my first shock at age five. During one of my nightly prayers I suddenly had the overwhelming feeling that I was praying to a vacuum. With eyes closed and hands clasped, I looked for an answer from God and saw nothing. I felt as if I were standing on the edge of an abyss. Darkness yawned before me; if there was a God, he wasn't answering me. I stretched out with all my senses, but there wasn't a shred of anything there, no special feeling, nothing to indicate a presence or response.

So after years of faithful prayer, I realized that God had never answered my prayers, at least not in a way I could understand or grasp. I felt no anger, just disappointment. I realized that I had been looking for spiritual contact and hadn't found it. If God existed, then I wasn't aware of Him. Somehow, despite following all the good advice from Good News Club, I had failed.

1.3.3   First Awareness of the Possibility of Awakening

Despite my disappointment in the Christian teachings as espoused in Good News Club, I continued to attend Sunday school, mostly at the urgings of my parents, although also to satisfy my continuing curiosity about all things spiritual. There I developed a reputation as someone who asked difficult questions. I didn't systematically search for answers, but often challenged existing beliefs and wondered about the origin of things. I sometimes stared hard at trees and wondered how they could be there before me, where they'd come from and why. I was also bothered by the fact there were so many different religions and even denominations within a given religion, and couldn't understand how they could all be true. They all seemed to require belief, and held those beliefs to be of utmost importance, but I'd tried that route and had found myself face to face with a void.

In the same year as my loss of faith I came across a reference to Buddha in my sixth grade history book. The reading was a great simplification of Buddha's message, suitable for sixth graders. The book told the following story of Buddha's awakening: He was meditating under a Bo tree, and when by chance his eye alighted on the planet Venus, he attained enlightenment and proclaimed: "Lo! All beings, by their very nature, are enlightened!"

That last line is a direct quote; it made such a powerful impression on me that I remember it clearly to this day. I found the declaration fascinating but had no idea what it meant. I knew only that enlightenment was some kind of special understanding. Ten years later I was sure that the statement was naive and wrong. Twenty years after that I realized it was profound and true.

But that night and many subsequent nights I stared at Venus in the night sky. In my child's mind I felt considerable affinity for the world, partly because I was keenly interested in astronomy and partly because my last name and the planet's name shared a common first letter. How intriguing that the mere observation of that shining world could perhaps stimulate some fabulous understanding of the universe! But no matter how long I looked, nothing happened, and I gave up. I resolved, however, that after graduating from college I would look into understanding what Buddha understood, if only to complete my education.

1.3.4 Teenage Confusion

I found the years following sixth grade especially difficult. An excellent student in grade school, I immediately foundered in disappointment and disillusionment when I started junior high school. I began ignoring my teachers and their attempts to educate me.

School was a trial, the students insensitive to each other, the classes boring and pointless. From being interested in everything I became interested in nothing. I'm not sure why this happened. I recall that I'd been very excited about going to junior high school because I anticipated learning exciting new things about the world, about the nature of things, about science. I also recall a deep feeling of disappointment after only a few days. Here I wanted to understand life, the universe, and everything, and instead I was diagramming sentences. On my first report card I made straight C's. Everyone was disappointed and no one could understand why it was happening. At the time I didn't understand it, either.

So I turned completely off to my formal education and daydreamed through my classes until my graduation from high school, playing a lot of competitive chess, the piano and guitar, reading books, but ignoring my classwork. I went to college at the urgings of my parents and flunked out. Physically I was not feeling well at all, but wasn't sure why. I went home a failure and began working odd jobs. My friends had all become hippies and I tried to be like them, but was a failure at that, as well. No matter how hard I tried, I just wasn't cool.

1.3.5 A Natural High

Subsequent to flunking out of college and hippie training school, I went through a period of fumbling through my relationships and dead-end jobs, dropping in and out of school, working in the mail room at the St.Petersburg Times, delivering pizza, teaching swimming lessons. I was living at home with my parents and not getting anywhere.

At nineteen one of my best friends introduced me to Zen Buddhism and the possibility of transformation through understanding. "Why don't you try a natural high?" he said with a grin as he strode along the sidewalks of Florida Presbyterian College, carrying a zen cushion under his arm. My response: "You mean there is one?"

Following my friend's lead, I got into meditation and yoga. It was the time of the Vietnam War and burned out hippies were trying to shock their parents and the establishment by embracing exotic beliefs and practices. I had a completely different motivation, however. I knew that I was unhappy and confused. I was lost. I was ready to try anything that might help me get my act together.

So I got involved with a Buddhist group, and practiced yoga and meditated hours every day for about a year, reading everything I could find on all the different religions, even different views of Christianity. I went on meditation retreats. I became infatuated with various authors and systems, but nothing quite seemed to click. There was always too much culture and not enough substance, and too often I just felt I was going through the motions without any real understanding. Some systems, such as certain sects of Buddhism, seemed very deep but I wasn't really sure, because while I could discuss abstractly all the intellectual aspects at length, I knew deep down that I didn't know what I was talking about. Other systems were appealing mainly because they were exotic. Fundamentally I had a hard time trusting religious authorities. It always seemed to me they ought to have a day job.

The regular meditation resulted in my experiencing a state called samadhi on two occasions. I describe this powerful experience in detail in a later essay. The experience is about as subtle as a roller coaster ride: spectacular and deeply thrilling. During this same period I also experienced numerous relatively weak flashes of insight.

At twenty my kidney disease, from which I'd suffered all my life, nearly killed me. After a couple of brushes with death, surgery and rigorous daily yoga greatly improved my health. The bad kidneys also got me out of going to Vietnam, so there was a silver lining of sorts. I returned to school, eventually getting back into science. All of a sudden I was an excellent student again, as I had been in elementary school. To make a long story short, I picked up where I'd left off at age eleven, becoming a scientist.

1.3.6   Fracturing the Cycle

Years of training in physics and mathematics developed my capacity for critical thinking. Although I enjoyed the work, I didn't know quite what I was getting into. I spent two decades just struggling to develop some kind of a career in science after my slow start. From time to time I still sat in formal meditation and did some yoga three or four times a week. I got married, completed a doctorate in physics, got a job, and then added two children and much later a third. I never forgot my spiritual quest, but it seemed life was passing me by. Like everybody else, I was too wrapped up in surviving, in my work, in where I was going.

Sometime soon after my fortieth birthday the cycle fractured. Paradoxically, the event occurred behind the steering wheel of a car, not sitting in lotus under a Bo tree. In a single moment while driving my old green Volvo the world turned inside out. It was amazingly deep and simple, stunningly obvious, and totally unexpected. In that instant I understood love for the first time in my life. I also saw that the naive characterization of Buddha's enlightenment in my sixth grade history book was true. Enlightenment was in everyone's nature; it was only necessary to awaken what was already there. I had to write it all down, it was too important to keep it to myself. This book came from that moment.

Since that time I have continued the quest. A common misconception is that such experiences transform your life and get rid of your problems. They do, indeed, transform the way you view the world, but your problems don't go away. Your ability to work with them, however, is considerably enhanced. Understanding and discovery happen in the present moment only, which means the quest, in a sense, never ends.

1.4   The Oracle

At this writing the year is 2012, which means some twenty years have passed since I decided to write this book. Since then, I've taken up the writing project numerous times and abandoned it just as many times. The story has always seemed too personal to share outside my immediate circle of family and friends, and given my many imperfections I was concerned that I might give inaccurate or incomplete information, or wrong impressions.

It turns out that when it comes to helping others, perfection is not a requirement. You can help others even if you have as yet plenty of unanswered questions. Many years passed before I understood this simple fact. It dawned on me while patiently listening to the rantings of a somewhat deranged old man at an auto repair shop. He was talking, making little sense, but I was listening and learning, gaining valuable perspective, insight into the human condition. I realized that even if I should inadvertently mislead someone in some small way, I could still render a valuable service.

So I invite you to read what I've written, and remember that I am imperfect, just like you are. Unlike a lot of self-help books, I'm going to do my best to give you the straight story, practical knowledge that you can apply in your daily life to make yourself happier, healthier, and more productive. I'm not going to write an abstract thesis, intellectually projecting what I think is true, or what I think works. I'm not going to promote a belief system, nor will I simply regurgitate the opinions of others. I'm just going to tell you what I understand, what I have grasped through my personal experience and direct perception.

Many self-help books start from a philosophy, a particular slant. While many of these philosophies may be helpful, they create a framework and try to put everyone else in it. That's fine, as far as it goes. It's reassuring to think that such a framework may exist, particularly if you happen to be an adherent of what you think is the correct philosophy. But it turns out that these frameworks, these philosophies, and systems of religious thought are of little intrinsic value. You don't need to study them. You don't need to know anything at all about them. I assure you, if truth exists, and it does, each and every one of you can see it for yourself. And, as you'll find out in this book, you don't really need me or anyone else to help you.

You are the oracle.

In the final analysis you've got to understand it for yourself. The books, the workshops, the retreats, the mantras and prayer beads, the Sunday potlucks will not necessarily help you understand anything. In most cases such social activities just provide a distraction from your everyday humdrum life, somewhere to spend your leisure time and hard-earned money. Those distractions are comforting because you feel that you're making progress and because you get a lot of positive strokes from others who are just as confused as you are. Surreptitiously, you may even decide you don't really have to put forth much effort.

Then one day, if you're fortunate, you wake up and realize you've been kidding yourself. You're still a mess, your life is a mess, you're like a puppet on two dozen strings, pulled this way and that by ill-understood impulses. You're hurting. It's finally time, you realize, to try putting your house in some semblance of order.

And you are perfectly capable of doing so by yourself.

At this point you might wonder, after all I've said, just what I have to offer. I've admitted the existence of my imperfections and the limits to my knowledge. I've even indicated you will have to understand things for yourself. That being the case, what are you going to get out of reading this book?

You may get nothing out of it. On the other hand, you may get something completely unexpected, something you never knew you were looking for, something you always had. A good modern analogy is the story of Dorothy and the Ruby Slippers in the Wizard of Oz. At the end of the tale the good witch Glinda, speaking of Dorothy's desire to return home, says: "She's always had the power, she just had to learn it for herself."

The witch is right.

So that's what we're going to do: go back home, back to what we already are. Our world is incredibly rich and diverse, full of light and colors, thoughts and feelings, sounds, textures, touches, and smells. Our everyday life is far more vivid and compelling than any imagined state of exotic consciousness. Yet because we have created a division in our consciousness, we're cut off from our world, experiencing only a filtered imitation of conscious living. And try as we might, we can't seem to get that special experience that will signal we've understood, that we've arrived. What do we do? How do we get there from here?

Actually, it's very simple: Everyday life is the special spiritual experience we're seeking.

That's right: Our life is already spiritual. We've just gone to great lengths to convince ourselves that it isn't.

There's more: Everything we experience is what we are.

Where are you? You are right here, right now. What are you? You are a magnificent evolving moment, a world that is constantly changing. Who are you? You are part of the whole, an artist, conductor and audience, designing and orchestrating the evolving moment.

I know you and I believe in you. The mere fact that you're still reading tells me that your potential is vast. You have a thirst for truth, for uncovering the understanding that will make a better life for you and everyone else. I couldn't care less about the past, what you have or haven't done, all that imaginary broken wreckage of good intentions, bad relationships, irreparable mistakes, and general confusion. I know all about that, because I've been there, and just like you I'm still slogging through the morass of everyday problems. I know you've struggled and suffered from your mistakes, just as I have.

We can put that all aside, now, because we're finally going to do something about it.

Chapter 2

Overview of a Human Life

2.1   First Years

We start our lives as chemical potentials in the form of separate egg and sperm, which unite to form an embryo in our mother's womb. Most of us don't remember very much prior to our birth, although we are certainly learning and developing at that stage. We grow inside our mothers, listening to the outside world through amniotic fluid and several layers of moist tissue. Both our physical body and our character are developing, and that development is strongly influenced by the environment provided by our mothers and less directly by our fathers.

Nine months later we're born into the world, often with a lot of difficulty, pain, and blood. If we're fortunate we have good parents who are motivated to love and care for us, and who have sufficient knowledge and plain good luck to provide for our needs. If we're like most people in the world, however, we're born into poverty, and our outlook is rather grim. Only a century ago the life expectancy was no more than about thirty-five years even in the developed countries. Today that's still a fairly ripe old age in much of the world.

Some of us will have childhood diseases, and suffer and die before ever growing up. Others will have genetic illnesses that impair our ability to function properly. Life will be dominated by struggle, frustration, loss, and pain.

The rest of us will develop more or less normally, and be more or less well taken care of, thanks to mother love, an extremely powerful instinct which makes it possible for children to survive even the most squalid conditions. Mother's milk and mother's love are the two most important and essential ingredients early in life, and we need to get as much as we can. If we're exceptionally fortunate, our fathers also shower us with attention.

As growing infants, we react in a very natural and raw way to the world. When we're hungry, we cry. When we're happy, we coo. Everything is spontaneous and unexpected, surprising, delightful and terrifying. During our first couple years we learn most of the essential skills needed for the rest of our lives:

language, socializing, and basic roles. Later experience may affect our character, but attitudes develop early, partly springing from genetic predisposition, partly from the way our parents interact with us. This is a difficult period, because we are powerless except for our ability to trigger instinctive responses in our caretakers, especially our mothers. It's also difficult because there's so much to learn, mainly by trial and error and by accident.

2.2   Walking and Talking

As we learn to walk and talk and get around on a limited basis, our parents reduce in size. Previously they filled our world when they were there, and created a terrible vacuum when they were not. Now that we have a certain amount of independence, their importance is slightly reduced. We begin exploring other people and other things. Parents provide our anchor in the enormous, frightening world, and we depend on them for sustenance and guidance. At the same time, we frequently test their power over us, because we have a will of our own and would like to know just how much we can get away with. It's a necessary part of growing up and becoming independent, and we both crave and fear the inevitable separation.

As we enter school and join large numbers of other children, new pressures are brought to bear on us. Now we have to learn to socialize with other children who are often impolite and highly self-centered, just as we are. This new environment creates both hazards and opportunities. The relationships are made complicated by the lack of maturity of our classmates and the fact that there are so many of them. Temporarily cut off from our secure caretakers, we're desperate for allies. We begin to modify our world view and self-image to match the opinions fed us by our peers. We desperately want to belong, and don't mind doing whatever is necessary to accommodate our new-found friends. Imitation is instinctual, as most parents quickly discover. Like little monkeys, we do whatever we see anyone else doing. Before going to school, we had mainly our parents to imitate. Now we can imitate a lot of other mixed-up kids.

In school we have a number of opportunities to get our feelings hurt. Some of us don't seem to have much in the way of feelings, while others among us are very sensitive in an emotional way. Much of this is built into our genes, and some is training. On the positive side, there's a lot of fun to be had developing friendships independent of the family circle. Those friendships help form and reinforce the self-image we've been putting together since before birth. We like people who admire us and respond to us in a positive way, and dislike those who make fun of us or hurt us. Our self-image is very fragile throughout childhood and even beyond; we've hardly learned to put it together and haven't yet become fluent in the use of defenses to maintain it properly. By the end of elementary school, however, most of us think we know who we are.

2.3   Young Adulthood

Then, just when we thought we understood ourselves, puberty steps in and slaps us in the face. Hormones start to surge. We begin to get a lot of pressure to grow up, get experience and become more independent. During this period those who are different are often ostracized, even if the difference is small. Our instinct is to fit in at all costs, so we try to imitate our friends so we won't be alone. We have to be liked by everyone, and the smallest things may prey on our minds, so that temporary inconveniences like skin blemishes will magnify into hideous deformities, both in our own minds and in the minds of our peers. Fun, excitement, struggle, and heartache are mixed in similar proportions.

During this period we may begin to turn on our parents, seeing them as the cause of many of our social problems. Conflict and alienation then result. We don't feel that anyone understands us. The real problem is that we don't really understand ourselves, because when we truly understand ourselves, it hardly matters if anyone else understands us or loves us. When we're most confused, however, the love and understanding of others is of gargantuan importance.

Despite this desire for love, we may embrace behavior patterns that make us hard to love. To a large extent this rebellion is instinctive, because otherwise we might never break away and become independent. A little mutual misunderstanding between parents and their children can ease the anxiety of separation.

Puberty is also when we usually begin collecting our first sexual experiences. Most of us inherit the discomfort and taboos of our parents, which are transmitted semi-consciously to us during our early years. That makes it difficult to talk about our sexual feelings. Even if we don't have any particular qualms, our peers do, so talking openly about our feelings may subject us to ridicule, creating a negative feedback that closes us up. As a result, we often remain ignorant of sexuality, its social contexts, and its consequences. Somehow we've got to get the information on our own. Sex is exciting partly because it's a return to infancy: once again, another person assumes literally a large portion of our landscape. And because we're inexperienced, we don't have much perspective on character and could end up in a tight squeeze with someone who later turns out to be something of a jerk.

Yet the pressure is on to perform, to be grown up about it. Teenagers know everything, and with their new-found omniscience they've decided their parents are hopelessly old-fashioned.

The truth, of course, is that our parents went through what we're going through, and they're doing their often inadequate best to protect us from the pain they experienced. But our emotions and hormones are pulling our strings and we're not about to take advice from anyone. There's no time to listen to advice, much less take it: our genes and our mixed up feelings are prodding us to action.

So it appears to be natural, although perhaps unnecessary nor always required, to go through a period of rebellion against parental love and authority. That period lasts roughly from the ages of about twelve to twenty-one, during which time we may seem to be doing our best to make serious mistakes, all the while collecting a number of pleasant and unpleasant experiences. It's a major struggle to put the finishing touches on *defining* who we are, which seems to be far more important than *understanding* who we are.

2.4   First Independence

Once we begin working a job and completely support ourselves, our attitude towards our parents, and that of our parents towards us, usually changes dramatically. We start to appreciate the environment of safety our parents created for us and can't resent them so much because, after all, we're on our own and doing what we want, more or less. Now the problem is that it didn't work out quite like we thought it would. We've got a whole world of people to get along with rather than just two people who love and care for us.

Serious relationships begin to intervene. We fall in love and become completely vulnerable to the dictates of our genes. Our DNA wants us to go forward with the program, which is reproduction. Character is not so much of a concern as long as the prospective mate appears to have the right stuff. Forget compatibility, we're talking about survival of the race, and for the guys, good legs and a nice body indicate a healthy specimen, which is basic to the business of procreation and surviving. For the ladies, a man with a good job and a nice disposition are strong attractants because pregnancy and child-rearing is a serious responsibility, and having a good, steady provider and partner is important. Our genes know the score and will pull our strings to fulfill their very obvious agenda.

The romance is fun, dizzy, better than the puppy love of puberty. The significant other person takes on gargantuan dimensions, a Rhodes astride the strait of Gibraltar. We are positively drunk with emotion, and our DNA keeps the juices pumping, building for the climax that will signal mission accomplished. But we're only dimly aware of all this behind-the-scenes manipulation; we're having the time of our lives, and we'll worry about the consequences later.

Then one of us gets pregnant, and we realize that we can't be totally self-centered any more. We've got to work hard to provide for a wailing, helpless baby who won't take no for an answer. Our children are causing the same problems for us as we caused for our own parents. Further, our spouse is either busy working or raising the children or both, and can't pay as much attention to us anymore. We shrink in importance.

Now, if we're like roughly half of all families in many countries, the pressures of life will split us apart, and divorce will be the result. Divorce is a major trauma, even when the problems are so great that it may be the only good answer.

On the other hand, if we're fortunate, we'll have a reasonably good marriage. Gradually the fights will subside and we will find a steady equilibrium with our spouses, adjusting to their quirks and caprices, finding some way to moderate our own, our children forming a bond of love and responsibility between us. Life can be so complex, in fact, that it's often easier to ignore the problems than to make things worse by addressing them.

2.5 Midlife Mayhem

As our children grow up, midlife crises begin to hammer away at us. We're approaching forty-something, and we've managed to put together a career and partly raise our children, when suddenly we realize that at least half our life is gone and we don't know where it went, it happened so fast. And the other half of our life looks like it's downhill the rest of the way. Our parents are beginning to fall to pieces, going into nursing homes, losing their minds to Alzheimer's, and maybe we have a brother with AIDS. Maybe it's been years since we had any good sex with our significant other person. We're bored out of our minds, and see that we haven't much time left, especially because, due to a kind of special relativity, time flows more quickly the more years we accumulate. Our options are beginning to narrow.

Desperate, we might begin to lash out, quit our jobs, think about leaving our spouses and kids. Maybe we'll buy a Harley motorcycle and roar off into the sunset. Why be responsible, when the final reward is rotting in a nursing home, drooling uncontrollably and filling our diapers? Escape becomes paramount, and this often results in more pain and suffering for ourselves and our families.

If we're fortunate enough to make it through this stage, we enter a more sedate middle age, where we care for aging parents and send our own children off into the world to fend for themselves. About this time, we begin to notice that it's much tougher staying in shape, and that various aches and pains are becoming commonplace. Small cuts, which long before healed in an afternoon or overnight, might take three or four days to close. We can't eat like normal people anymore, unless we want to put on the soft stuff. Every ounce of french fries seems to translate into a pound of slack.

2.6 Old Age, Disease, and Death

Finally our parents die, and we're truly on our own. We keep in touch with our children, and relive our youth vicariously through them and their families. As our bodies decline, we begin to get more serious about religion, and participate more in rituals. For some of us, this stage may have happened much earlier; the time it commences varies widely. Seeing the suffering around us and anticipating more hard times ourselves, we hope that through belief of one kind or another we can ensure our future safety and well-being, or at least come to terms with what looks like a no-win situation.

If we are unfortunate, we fall prey to disease. We'll be diagnosed as having prostate cancer or breast cancer and have to undergo operations. Then we'll have to get used to living with the dread of reoccurrence, or perhaps to living without a limb or with some dysfunctional organ. Even if major disease doesn't strike, the aches and pains will get greater, more insistent. We'll start stocking up on pain relievers and other medicines. At best, we'll experience a slow decline some twenty or thirty years long, during which our physical capacity will gradually diminish. Somewhere along the way we might have to care for an ailing spouse or grown child.

Finally we'll get too old and sick to care for ourselves. We'll have to enter a hospital or nursing home, or lay around at home being cared for by our children. There won't be much left but the memories of our pleasures, of our small triumphs, but those will be fading fast.

If we're lucky, death will come quickly and easily; however, it's often long, cruel, and hard.

2.7   Summary Analysis

The foregoing description may seem to ignore the good and focus on the bad, but it's a reasonable depiction of what many of us have to endure, if we're among the more fortunate. Of course there are good times and bad, and then the long slide. But it is also true that there are some countries, torn by political and economic chaos, where life is just a matter of day-to-day survival. Happiness doesn't enter the equation.

The point of this description is to lay out what everyone knows already, without equivocation. The human condition is what we're dealing with, and while ignoring the problems can dull the pain, it's counterproductive. The situation we're facing is serious, and we should do our best to optimize our response to it. Some may call this self-centered, but it's important to realize that you are a large part of your world. If you can take better care of yourself and your problems, you and everyone around you will be a lot better off.

Now, many religions focus on the afterlife, and there are reports that there may indeed be some existence beyond death. Most of us don't have memory of previous lives, and only little knowledge of the reports of any afterlife, so it isn't really practical to address that particular issue. What should interest us is what we are: living beings with problems to be faced on a daily basis.

So here is what we must work with: a life that is a series of challenges, full of strife, heartache, fleeting pleasures and joys. And we must adjust to growing old, becoming infirm, and finally dying. In the end, everything we worked so hard to achieve will be taken away from us.

That sounds like a no-win situation, but in fact it means our focus needs to be elsewhere. The experiences and the things we accumulate will all be forfeit, so logically we shouldn't make such pursuits the point of our existence. What is important is not what we accumulate over time, but the quality of our experience in each and every moment. Seeing this, it's natural to turn to someone else, some spiritual authority, and let them tell us what is meaningful. Such people can be helpful, but it's important to realize that their understanding is not necessarily ours, and that they could very well be as confused as we are.

Fortunately, our confusion is our ally and guide on a fantastic voyage of discovery. Our lives may be drab, and sometimes difficult, but in that rocky soil lie the seeds of awakening to what we are. And what we are is a fantastic vista beyond the reach of time. Each one of us is an oracle, a pathway leading onwards and upwards, towards profound understanding and light.

Chapter 3

The Nature of Consciousness

It's always best to start in the beginning, and the beginning for all of us is consciousness. It's also the end and everything in between. It turns out that understanding consciousness is key to understanding ourselves, our problems, and our world. So that's where we're going to start. It took me more than forty years before I came very suddenly to the understanding of consciousness I describe here. I can't say for sure whether the four decades preceding that understanding prepared me in any way. I believe that such understanding can happen in forty years or forty seconds.

3.1 The Oracle

What is the nature of consciousness? Related questions include: Who am I? Where am I? Why? Scientists, philosophers, psychologists, and religious leaders have all tried to answer those questions, and now it's our turn. Where do we start? Whom do we turn to? It's normal not to have the slightest idea. Maybe you've tried a few different philosophies or religious groups, and now you're trying me. I'd like to suggest that you try someone else.

Yourself.

Maybe that's too radical. Aren't we supposed to find someone more knowledgeable and learn from that person? Alternately, why not develop an inventory of all prior speculations and opinions, religious and otherwise, then choose the one that best resonates with what we already believe to be true? That's what most people do. They collect pleasant-sounding phrases, some good cocktail party chatter, and then sit back and hope it will do them some good.

On the other hand, maybe we've had enough of that. Maybe we're ready to find out the real answers for ourselves. If so, let's start by putting all the old ideas aside, all of our preconceived notions of the nature of the self, universe, of religion, of philosophy. Let's start with a clean slate.

As stated earlier, I developed my first theory of consciousness on the kindergarten playground. When I asked myself where I was, that "I" was a given quantity. I was somewhere, and I wanted to know where and how I fit in. What was this place, this world, the trees, the shells, the grass and sky, and how did I come to be there?

As related earlier, I decided that I was inside my head peering out the windows of my eyes. That view is very common, and many people unconsciously adopt it. "You" are "in there", inside your head, and "out there" is the rest of the world. Your body is in between, a partner who helps make the connections between you and everything else.

Here's the reality: this picture of the world, of an internal you and an external world, is a fabrication.

That's a radical statement. How could it possibly be true? Does it mean that the trees and flowers and sky and sun are part of what we are? And even if that were the case and we could believe it, what would it imply? Is believing it the same as seeing or experiencing it?

I struggled with those and similar questions. In the end, of course, belief is not enough and does very little, although it might affect our actions in some positive way. Belief can be useful, or a crutch, or it can be harmful, but it isn't transforming. Knowing that transformation is possible, however, is always useful, because there are steps that can be taken that can increase the possibility of a spontaneous change. It's a matter of perception, not belief.

As we'll see, and contrary to what seems to be evidently true, the internal world and the external world are not separate. They coexist in the same field, the field of consciousness. Paradoxically, that consciousness isn't any special consciousness; it's just the ordinary everyday consciousness that we all have.

3.2   The Process of Perception

The first time I became aware that my childhood world view might not be the only one possible was in my college physics class, listening to a lecture on light. While the lecturer droned on about the physics of light, I began thinking about how photons, particles of light, bounce off objects, then enter the eye. There they stimulate the optic nerve, creating impulses that travel to the visual cortex and cause the perception of an image in the brain. It struck me that consciousness was indirect, always occurring through intermediate channels. When we see a tree, for example, we feel it is happening at some distance from us. It never occurs to us that what we're seeing is constructed in the visual cortex on the backside of our brain.

That particular perception and understanding was primarily intellectual, and aroused my curiosity, although it didn't affect me deeply. The old way of regarding the world was only slightly impacted, and I didn't think too much of the idea, not yet realizing its significance.

Some years later I was enjoying a pleasant Florida evening at my Gainesville apartment. I was a mathematics graduate student, living on my own. My keys were on the kitchen table, and as I reached for them something odd happened. The keys seemed intimately close, as if they weren't separate from me. I felt as if I were reaching for and grasping something that was part of me already, reaching for a fragment of my own consciousness. It was a strange and alien feeling that requires further discussion of the neurophysics of perception.

What goes into seeing a tree? As we've already discussed, light from the sun in the form of particles called photons reflects off the material substance of the tree. Most of the photons, of course, are absorbed or scattered at wide angles. Only some of them, those of particular colors, are scattered towards us. Those photons travel through space and enter the eye, striking the retina. Stimulated, the optic nerve then transmits signals to the visual cortex located on the backside of the brain. The brain cells in the visual cortex process the signals and construct from them a detailed picture of the objects the photons bounced off, often with considerable input from memory and other cognitive faculties.

We then reach out with our hand and point at that image, which is purely a mental construct, and say, "There's a tree over there". Our perception of our hand, of course, is a similar mental construction, and of our arm, our body, and everything else in the picture. So in a sense we never really see anything at all. We only see a representation created by our own brain.

A simple scientific proof that our brains are putting the visual world together is the fact that the image on our retinas is actually upside down. The brain takes that upside down image and makes it seem right-side up. Psychologists have done experiments where subjects wear special glasses that flip everything upside down. The image on the retina is now right-side up, but the brain sees it as upside down. After a few confusing days of wearing the glasses, however, everything seems right-side up again. The brain makes the adjustment.

Other senses work in a similar way. The brain creates a virtual reality that aids us in interacting with our "true" environment. So the keys we see on the kitchen table are not "out there", on the table, but rather "in here" along with all the other perceptions and sensations and bubbling thoughts. Our brain takes the raw incoming sensations carried by our nerves and creates a perception out of them. We become conscious of this created perception rather than of the original object itself.

Our consciousness, therefore, comes to us through our senses, our nerves, through something akin to a virtual reality constructed by our brain. That means we have no direct contact whatsoever with the so-called exterior world. Such direct contact is a physical impossibility.

Yet here's a further observation: the idea that everything is happening in our mind is just as erroneous as thinking it happens in some exterior world.

That is an outrageous statement. We've just convinced ourselves that everything is happening in our mind, and now the claim is that's wrong, too. How could both viewpoints be wrong? It's wrong because there can't be an inside without an outside. Saying that consciousness is happening "in here", in our minds inside our heads, is just as wrong as saying that the trees, clouds, the sun, and so forth, are "out there", exterior to us. Our "interior world" is just as much a created virtual reality as our "exterior world".

Just about everyone intuitively believes in the apparent reality of the interior world, but it's an artificial construct. The interior and exterior worlds constitute a single field, the field of consciousness, the very ordinary consciousness that everyone has.

Now, at this point, we are discussing something intellectually, using words and memory to string together some ideas. That's very different from actually *perceiving* the world as an indivisible whole. When your world view goes through a sudden transformation and you see it directly, it will literally be like going from blindness to sight. The same content of consciousness can be viewed dualistically or nondualistically, but the two experiences are very different. Dualistically, the experience may seem limited or small, muted, whereas the same experience viewed nondualistically is a fantastic vista.

3.3   Thought Experiments

The absence of separation between our interior and exterior worlds can be called non-duality, or "not dual", "not two". Now, everything in our everyday experience seems to refute a non-dual view of the world. Back when I had only my first glimpses of this non-dualistic perception it was easy to get confused by amateur philosophers armed with hypothetical situations.

Thought Experiment 1: Suppose Jack and Jill devise the following experiment. Jill goes inside a house, leaving Jack outside. Inside, out of sight and sound of Jack, Jill rearranges the furniture. She then goes back outside and asks Jack what changes have been made. Jack has no idea. Jill then claims that this is conclusive proof that there is an exterior world separate from Jack's interior world, for otherwise Jack would know how the furniture was rearranged.

Jill's argument appears irrefutable. Others are capable of independent action, and if everything were happening in our minds, then it seems we'd know about it. But there's a completely different way of looking at this situation. What has been proven in this thought experiment is that the fragment of consciousness called Jack is not omniscient. Jack doesn't know everything, and why should he? Parts of the whole other than Jack have rearranged the furniture, that's all. That he is unaware of the new arrangement is no more surprising than the fact he isn't aware of all the numerous processes taking place in his own body. Cells die and get carted off by the millions. Other cells grow. Trillions of rearrangements of the cellular constituents occur daily. Jack is ignorant of all this. Carrying the logic forward, we would have to conclude that Jack and his body, even his brain, are separate from Jack himself, something most people would deny as nonsensical.

In other words, you can be part of something and that something can be part of you whether or not you have any personal control over it. So the answer to this thought experiment is that what we identify as our personal self, whether it is body, mind, or spirit, is only a fragment of the totality of our own everyday consciousness. Lack of omniscience on the part of one fragment doesn't mean it's separate from the rest.

A good analogy can be found in the different bodily organs, which work together and independently towards a common goal. The heart doesn't know what the lungs are doing, but that doesn't matter. Different organs take care of different functions, just as different people take different roles in the creation of our universe.

Thought Experiment 2: Jill fires a gun point blank at Jack and kills him. She lives, he dies. If there is truly no separation between Jack and the rest of the universe, why did Jack allow himself to be killed? And why didn't the universe die with him? That refutes the idea that self and universe are not separate.

The second thought experiment baffled me for a long time. A fragment of the world, Jill, has created a situation that appears to radically contradict the idea of a single field of being. What could be more proof than having someone shoot you, followed by your dropping dead? On the other hand, how is murder different from, say, contracting an auto-immune disease? Just as there is no guarantee our bodies will remain healthy and free of disease, there is similarly no guarantee the other fragments of our life, such as the other people, are going to always act in our personal best interests. Just as we don't completely control our bodies and minds, so also do we only incompletely control our environment.

The point here is that our personal self is only one part of the whole, the totality of being. The totality is just the totality of our consciousness at any given moment. Perceiving this directly, and not just intellectually, is non-dual perception. Nondual perception is not the same thing as omnipotence or omniscience. A person is only part of his own whole; he doesn't control all aspects of that whole. A similar fallacy would be to argue that because the heart is not separate from the body, then it must also be able to think, breathe, and perform all the functions of the other body parts, but of course it can't. An organ is part of a whole, and has a range of functions and limitations, and similarly a person is part of a whole, and is similarly limited.

Other preconceptions are also at work in this thought experiment. People have the notion that when they're dead the world continues on without them, thus proving the existence of an exterior and separate world. The continuance of the rest of the world after we die, of course, is pure speculation, a function of the intellect, in particular of memory. If we're dead and presumably unconscious, then we have no way of verifying whether the world goes on or not. And, as far as we're concerned the world went away with us.

By the way, does the world go on after we die?

We see other people die, and the world doesn't cease to exist for us, so we *surmise* that when we die, the material world will similarly continue on for others. That knowledge comes to us through memory and intellect rather than direct perception.

So the fact that there is no true separation between inside and outside doesn't mean we personally have control of everything. We don't even control our own thoughts, nor our heartbeats, nor a billion other little details that happen continuously in our bodies. It all happens automatically, just as the universe, seamlessly joined to us, functions without our pushing it. That's part of its beauty: it's not perfect, but all in all it works extremely well.

Up to this point, we've used the word *totality* several times, and it's important to understand what is meant by it. The word can invoke a vision of the vast extent of the material universe, stars, planets, and galaxies throughout infinite space. That vision is just a projection, however, a function of our imagination. The true meaning of totality is more fundamental. The totality is what we perceive here and now, including whatever is happening in our mind. Anything beyond that, like the Andromeda Galaxy, is also there, but is happening in our imagination.

Try the following experiment. Close your eyes and listen to the sounds around you. Then listen to the inner sounds, the thoughts, fragments of music that may be arising randomly through your brain. The outer sounds and the inner sounds are very similar. The main difference is that the outer sounds are usually more intense, and a certain physical sensation in the general location of the ear is experienced, and sometimes elsewhere.

So when we hear a sound, or experience a touch, or look at a tree, we are not observing something separate from us. We are observing a fragment of our consciousness, one piece of the grand representation, the virtual reality our brain is creating with the assistance of the senses and the so-called external world.

It's natural to be confused by this discussion, and it's also natural to suspect that it's all a lot of nonsense. That's normal and healthy skepticism at work. Most people, myself and many others, have found this unified view of the world to be perplexing and frustrating as long as it remained solely on the intellectual level. When you really see it, however, it's stunning and surprising, but at the same time very natural and normal. In that moment and for that moment, your world is whole. You see the beauty in ugliness and the energy in being when by accident or grace the barriers you erected fall away.

3.4   Consciousness

We have established, at least intellectually and provisionally, that there is effectively no separate inner world, nor separate outer world. Pragmatically, of course, we believe there is and function accordingly, but as far as what we experience, there's only that virtual reality, the only reality, where everything's happening together. What, then, is consciousness? What is its nature?

Consciousness is what you are conscious of, everything you sense, feel, think about, the car passing down the road, the bird singing on the branch, the wind against your body, your breath passing in and out, the sun and moon and stars. All these things, either as direct perceptions or as memories, constitute your consciousness, and nothing more.

That realization was personally very surprising to me because throughout my life, whenever I regarded, say, a tree, I always had an impression of the tree being "over there", spatially separated from me. I always thought I was seeing a physically distinct and separate object, and it never occurred to me that in fact a very creative process was making that perception possible. The whole view of separateness was so thoroughly ingrained in my perceptual pathways that I couldn't see it any other way. The tree was over there, and I was over here. Such a divided worldview was not open to question.

As it turns out, however, consciousness is not separate from the things we are conscious of. It can't be, because we create that consciousness. Everything we are conscious of constitutes our world, and there's nothing outside of it, inside of it, or beyond it. That means that if we're interested in a better understanding of consciousness, then we can't miss. It's everywhere.

Most people have a vague feeling that consciousness is somehow associated with the head. We look across a lake and see a sailboat, and we automatically consider it to be external, far away, separate, which it is, intellectually speaking. In reality, however, we are helping to create that perception of the sailboat, it's happening "in our brains", so it really isn't far away at all.

Here's a curious personal experience that I encountered early in my self-training in meditation. When you sit and relax deeply for some time, there is a tendency for the mind to become more sensitive to pressures and tensions in the scalp, among other places. Early in my training, when I arose from a session of cross-legged sitting, I would be acutely aware of my scalp. It felt almost as if I were wearing a football helmet. Naively, I thought this was my "consciousness" expanding beyond the confines of my body! In fact, my conscious perception was conducting business as usual. The trees were still "out there" along with the clouds and everything else, and I was still "in here" with my "expanded consciousness", which was in fact just an awareness of feeling in my scalp.

The lesson is that it's easy to become deluded by emotional experiences and by the interpretation of sensations, particularly when developing the kind of sensitivity that comes through deep calm and meditation. The consciousness we are trying to understand, however, is everywhere, in the most sublime and mundane experiences. What makes it difficult is that it's not the normal kind of understanding, such as the rules of calculus, but a transformation of perception. The word transformation is itself misleading, because you are simply becoming aware of what you already are. You have created the duality, the inside and outside, and the illusion is so complete that no other possibility seems to exist.

So we go about our lives, dealing with fragments of our consciousness, all the while thoroughly convinced that the fragments are separate. Only when the division ceases, if only for an instant, can the impact and beauty of nondual perception be realized.

3.5 Nonduality as a Logical Argument

Another way of persuading ourselves as to the possible reality of nondual perception is to consider the great philosophies of idealism and materialism. People often adopt one or the other of these two apparently disparate philosophies, sometimes unconsciously. Some may say that the non-dual world view is a form of idealism.

Idealists believe everything happens in the mind, that there is no separate reality. Our consciousness is everything, and there is nothing outside of it. I. B. Horner, the great translator of Buddhist texts from the original Pali, once expressed this opinion to me when I visited her in England. At the time I couldn't offer any alternative, although I privately thought she might not be correct. In any case, I didn't want to argue with a very elegant and kindly old lady. Idealism is a powerful idea, and there is a great deal of truth to it.

Materialists, on the other hand, believe the opposite: everything is put together in some objective way and is material in its origins. The mind and mental objects are governed by the properties of matter. There is a clear-cut objective reality that exists outside and beyond our consciousness, and is responsible for its existence.

As a physicist, I'm supposed to believe that the universe is strictly material and is governed by the laws of matter and energy. Indeed, it could be argued that without the actual material objects that create the sensations we perceive, it would be impossible to experience the sensations. From that point of view, therefore, objective material reality is absolutely essential. If there is no objective, material external reality, there is no consciousness. The contrapositive of this statement, which logically conveys the same meaning, is: If there is consciousness, then there is an external material reality.

On the other hand, without the mind and consciousness, it would be similarly impossible for the sensations to be experienced and the virtual reality constructed from them. Without consciousness, the external material world, for all intents and purposes, would not exist. The contrapositive of this statement is that if the external material world exists, then consciousness exists.

In other words, consciousness implies the existence of an external material world, which in turn implies the existence of consciousness. In logic, when one statement implies a second, and the second statement implies the first, then the two statements are equivalent. The material world that creates consciousness, therefore, is equivalent to the consciousness it creates. This simple logical argument implies there is no separating what we call our consciousness and what we call our world. Logically and actually they are equivalent.

Nonetheless, even a good logical argument can fail to dispel confusion created by the concept of nondual perception. There are numerous hypothetical scenarios, and in every case it's too easy to fall into our usual preconceptions. A good example of such a hypothetical scenario is the old puzzle about trees falling in forests. If a tree falls in a forest and there is no one around to hear it, is there a sound? A physics professor asked me this question when I was an undergraduate. I fell silent, thinking it over, and was frankly baffled. When I didn't answer immediately, he went on, saying, "Don't be ridiculous, of course there's a sound."

At that time I couldn't disagree, but the correct answer is both yes and no.

When a tree falls in the forest, there is a sound, but unless we're there, witnessing it, that sound occurs only intellectually, in our imagination, as a projection of our memory. Practically speaking, if we didn't physically hear it then there was no sound. In other words, the answer is "no". On the other hand, *based on our memory of prior experiences*, we know that had we been there in the forest when the tree fell, then we would have heard a sound. Looked at that way, the answer is "yes".

Projecting that there was a sound based on our remembered experience is distinct from the experience of actually hearing the sound, so in these separate senses, both answers can be considered correct. The tree fell in the forest, and it made a sound in our imagination.

A viewpoint similar to that of idealism is the concept of "oneness". This idea is distinct from the concept of non-duality, although for some it may only be a matter of semantics. Advocates of oneness sometimes have an idea that everything in the universe is connected together by a grand cosmic weave. Somehow, while everything appears separate, it's actually all made out of the same stuff, seething with *prana*, whatever that is, and when we're tuned in we can really see and feel these physical connections. "Cosmic consciousness" puts you in touch with the entire universe: not only your own body, but also the body of your next-door neighbor, the rocks, the grass, the trees, the sun, the moon, and the beings populating distant galaxies.

While it's true that certain states of consciousness, such as samadhi, may promote the unity interpretation, I have seen no particular evidence for oneness in the sense of sharing some kind of etheric circulatory system with everything there is. A nice idea, but I don't think it's necessary to buy into it, so I don't. It isn't hard, through a process similar to self-hypnosis, to generate feelings that simulate such a worldview. That, however, is just as much a delusion as the dualistic worldview.

The materialistic point of view, often adopted by scientists, diminishes the extremely important role of the mind. The idealistic point of view diminishes the importance of the material world. Both of these world views are incorrect because they deny the existence of the other. Further, it is even incorrect to say they are two aspects of the same phenomenon. They are identical and equivalent in every way.

Regardless, at the end of the day subscribing to either of materialism or idealism will have very little impact on our lives. Philosophies are the domain of the intellect and belief, whereas understanding is through direct perception. A nondual world view isn't a matter of choosing to believe it to be so. Belief is a function of memory, which is the past. When you consider that nearly forty years passed before the nondual worldview struck me with force, you can appreciate that such a transformation in perception is likely to be a rare event, not just a matter of faith.

Further, believing my words won't take you any closer to the truth. Believing might make you feel better, or it might give you some mental relief, and that's fine, as far as it goes. But when you observe directly that there is no separation between what you previously considered yourself and the so-called external world, something amazing happens. Stress levels drop drastically. You find yourself being generally friendly with all those around you. It gets harder to carry grudges against those who cause you problems. Simple activities such as washing the dishes can take on a new significance: a giddy kind of energy lights you up as you take another spoon out of the sink and see it directly as part of what you are.

A further benefit of the nondual worldview is that you stop taking yourself so seriously. Why should your right hand worry about trying to make a good impression on your left? There's not much point in it anymore. It's much easier to relax and be yourself. Life is less complicated. Salesmen and politicians have a harder time manipulating you.

When you see that all you experience lies in a single field, and that there is nothing beyond that field, then you truly understand nonduality and have in a real sense "cosmic consciousness", which is just the ordinary consciousness that you carry around with you, but with a transformed worldview. In that perception, prejudices vanish, as do anger and acquisitiveness. Everything is easier.

Having discussed all this, the natural question is the following: how do we acquire this fantastic view of the world? What does it feel like? Those details and more will be discussed in a later essay. Briefly, we arrive at this worldview spontaneously, as a result of the simple observation of our day-to-day stream of conscious experience. It turns out that memory, which is the past, puts a filter over our immediate perceptions, creating the division, which in turn saps our energy and drains the life out of our immediate experience.

When the past falls away, the present opens up like a flower to the rising sun. The world is fresh, vibrant, alive, and we're filled with love that is empowering and beautiful. We are a fantastic vista, a world full of mystery, beauty, light, and passion. That's our natural state. That's who we are.

Chapter 4

Habit Versus Insight

In the previous chapter we discussed nondual perception, which occurs in the absence of a separation between what we call our inner experience and our outer experience. Nondual perception has the power to transform life experience, greatly enriching it and reducing stress. The problem, then, is how to arrive at such a state of perception. This chapter is about two contrasting methods for uncovering this natural state of being. In one method, change is slowly effected through practice. In the second method, change can occur suddenly through insight.

4.1 Habit

Traditional religions tend to embrace the cultivation of habit, mainly because it's easiest. In this approach, changes are effected by a gradual modification of behavior. Through a communication of memory and experience, our sources of spiritual inspiration advise and encourage certain practices which are said to contribute to our long term well-being and that of our relationships. Whereas some are of the opinion that blind habit is a hindrance and should be avoided at all cost, healthy habits can simplify life, improve the sensitivity of the nervous system, and predispose the mind to insight. An extreme view on habit, either for or against, is unnecessary and possibly somewhat hazardous to our health.

Most people are raised in an environment that is religious to some degree. Even children of atheist households are taught certain modes of conduct and morality. Such training is essential to the raising of a productive and functional member of society. We tend to imitate our parents and our peers, conforming to their codes of behavior and appearance, suppressing and channeling our more fundamental impulses. After a while, such imitation becomes so ingrained that it seems to be a law of nature. Anyone acting outside of a certain range of behavior parameters is labeled strange, and is usually ostracized until the behavior is corrected. The appropriate behavior, often confused with virtue, is praised and encouraged.

There are many examples of habitual activity. Brushing our teeth, taking a certain route to work, eating certain foods at certain times are all habitual activities. Reading the newspaper and watching television can become habitual, as can attending religious services. In every case the activity feels natural. We don't think about it too much, but it feels right. Society conditions us to respond in certain ways, we condition ourselves to respond in certain ways, and we feel vaguely uneasy if we don't follow that conditioning. That feeling of vague uneasiness is fear: the fear of being different, the fear of change. When we perform the habitual activity, the fear goes away and we feel relief. The relief acts as a positive reinforcement for the behavior, allaying the insecurity and fear.

Habit can be useful. How many of us have had the experience of driving all the way from home to work, then suddenly realizing we were lost in thought and unaware of what we were doing for the entire half-hour of the trip? Our habitual reactions are extremely powerful and are often capable of carrying out complex tasks without our conscious control. That ability can allow us to focus on details of our work that would otherwise lie beneath notice. So habitual response is useful and even necessary. Without some training of the motor system, we couldn't drive cars or fly airplanes.

The problem with habit, however, is its potential for abuse. How is habit abused? Habit is often used to escape responsibility. With sufficiently trained habit, for example, we can carry out our duties mindlessly while daydreaming of something else. We're too lazy, too bored to pay attention to what we're doing, and why should we? We can do it while effectively asleep. A case in point is a certain priest who was so well-trained in his liturgy that he claimed he could deliver the entire ritual while thinking of something else entirely, just like the cab driver who whizzes along the crowded streets of New York without any conscious awareness of the conditions around him. The priest was proud of his talent, and other priests greatly admired him for it. It's also possible to do dishes, wash cars, or change diapers that way.

Now, it's natural to ask what's wrong with knowing an activity so well that we can let our bodies take over while we take a mental vacation from the drudgery?

The problem is not so much the habitual activity in itself. As we've seen, a certain amount of automatic pilot is useful and necessary. The problem is why we've created the habit, and continue to nurture it.

The answer, partly, is our desire for pleasant sensations. We wash the dishes automatically so that we can think about something else, something that will create a drone of pleasurable sensation in our nervous system. This background feeling we often identify as our self.

Try watching your feelings the next time you're doing the dishes while reflecting on, say, your tennis game or golf game, or what you're going to buy at the store. The selected train of thought is creating a subtle background of sensation which is basically pleasurable. We want these sensations and we identify with them, at least most of the time. The dark side of this kind of desire is when we are thinking about unpleasant things. The mechanism is the same, but now we are unwillingly absorbed in negative thoughts, which we wish to disown, eliminate, change. Rather than pleasurable, such thoughts are painful and distressing. And just as we can't break our habitual washing of dishes and habitual thinking of pleasant topics, we have similar problems dissociating ourselves from the unpleasant thoughts. They're two realizations of the same phenomenon. You can't have one without the other.

Habits are closely related to ritual behavior. Cloaking various facts of life in ritual is society's way of handling embarrassing or difficult everyday problems, or of maintaining control. Sex, for example, has been tremendously ritualized simply because of the power it holds over us, and the power it implies. The marriage rituals help people guide and harness the power of sex. Ideally, sexual feelings should be discussed and understood, but because the feelings are often so strong and private, it's difficult for many people to do so. Rituals are then used to provide guidance and control.

Habit isn't a virtue, only a simulation of virtue. A virtue is a strength, something spontaneous that springs from within. If we send flowers to communicate our love of a person we don't really care about, it isn't a virtue, it's a lie. If we act automatically, habitually, in giving our tithe every week to the church, it isn't a virtue, it's fear.

Rituals have sprung up throughout society, all for the express purpose of having some physical action fill the void within us. We need these rituals because without them there seems to be nothing there, no religion, no substance, no revelation. And these rituals, which are habits falsely endowed with deep meaning, strike chords within us, all because the traditions were established when we were young. Let's strip away all our habits, our habitual thinking, the things we like to regularly do. What's left?

On the other hand, why do we want to break our habits? What's wrong with them? Now that's a very interesting question, because here we enter another kind of evasion. We're driven by our habits, we're slaves of the past, and we don't like the way we are, so we contrive to change ourselves in some way that will result in our becoming someone we like and admire. Consequently, we replace our old habits with new habits! It's a vicious circle, but if we don't try to change our old habits, how can we improve?

Now here's the difficulty: many of our habits, like watching TV or reading the newspaper, are considerably more subtle than a hot stove. Even a habit such as smoking might not seem to be affecting us all very much. So we keep lighting up, destroying our health.

It's a question of sensitivity. By sensitivity I don't mean emotion or feelings, but physical sensitivity. Habits of any kind reduce our sensitivity to our minute-by-minute experience. But here's the catch: how can we be sensitive when we're slaves to habits that make us insensitive? How can we get the process rolling?

Here's the paradoxical answer: start cultivating healthy habits!

Just a moment ago we decided our habits are an escape from what we are, and because we're busy escaping from what we are, there is no chance that we'll understand ourselves just as we are, which is what we need to do to break those habits naturally. Now we're going to start cultivating habits in order to change, to transcend the habit-ridden lives we're leading. Isn't that a paradox?

The resolution of this paradox is simple. The nervous system is a two-way street. We have various feelings in our bodies which create thoughts and impulses, sometimes positive, sometimes negative. At the same time, thoughts and impulses, created in us by the actions and words of others or by our own actions, thoughts, or words, have the power to create various feelings in our bodies.

This is commonly known as a kind of self-hypnosis, the power of positive thinking. We can gently convince ourselves to change our ways simply by planting the seed in our conscious thought. Our unconscious brain, the one that controls our autonomous bodily processes, is not that smart when it comes to words and thoughts, and will tend to go along with whatever the conscious brain says. It just takes a little gentle persuasion.

Now, as we cultivate healthier habits, better hygiene, better diet, calmer thoughts, safer sex, and so forth we start becoming more physically sensitive. And as we become more physically sensitive, we gain the potential for deeper insight, which in turn helps those bad habits drop away like so much dead wood.

Naturally, a good shot of insight right at the outset would save us a lot of trouble, but most of us aren't going to be that lucky. We're too used to looking analytically at everything and don't have the patience to simply observe, and keep observing, without trying to draw some conclusion or create some illusory state of consciousness. Instead, we'd like to take one peek and then get something for it, a trophy experience or a permanent high. Something to write home about.

Now, how do you create a healthy habit? As stated above, it's basically a matter of persuasion.

If you want to quit smoking, for example, you could sit quietly for a few minutes every day, imagining yourself free of the habit, turning away from cigarettes with disgust, embracing healthy alternatives. Imagine your most probable future; lying in a hospital bed suffering from emphysema or lung cancer. Imagine your normally pink lungs looking dark, blackened from years of abuse. Do this every day. A good time is right before you go to sleep.

And, of course, it doesn't hurt to observe yourself in the act of reaching for a cigarette, lighting up and smoking. First there's a gnawing sense of dissatisfaction, then an onset of pleasure as you reach for your pack and withdraw one of the slender tubes. Taking out a pack of matches or a Bic butane, you light up with a flare, feeling like one of the tough guys on TV who lassos cattle and drives fast cars.

Images and imagination create subtle sensations that stand out from the background and direct our behavior. Any Madison Avenue advertising executive knows that. So why not choose the behavior you want and then make it happen? You have far more power over your feelings and everyday experience than you may think.

Now, a caveat: while you may wish to develop a healthier and happier lifestyle through proper imagination and self-suggestion, you should avoid the abuse of self control. We've all met people who are enormously self-disciplined, virtual tyrants over themselves. That kind of tyranny is something to be avoided. Bullying yourself may get a few quick results, but unfortunately can often create tremendous inner conflicts, negating any good that may otherwise have resulted from the disciplined behavior. Further, if you bully yourself often enough, there's a tendency to start bullying others, as well. After all, why should you cut them any slack when you don't cut it for yourself?

Moderation is the key. You don't have to be perfect, and if you were, nobody could stand you.

Now, how do you go about using imagination to help establish healthier habits? This will be taken up in greater detail in the chapter on meditation. Basically, (and this is as hard as it gets) you sit quietly and reflect on positive images. You might have a problem, for example, with fear or hate, which are closely related emotions. Maybe you're always very negative, seeing the dark side of every situation. To combat this, sit quietly and repeat, over and over, 'may I be happy'. Imagine yourself feeling happy, taking care of yourself. A lot of angry people have, at their core, a fundamental dislike for themselves. You can't love anybody else before you love yourself, so that's the purpose of wishing yourself happiness.

To overcome excessive lust, either for sex or other material things, it's not a bad idea to reflect on the parts of the body in an analytical way, and on the impermanence of the body. Think about how it gets older. Think about how the body you lust after will harangue you and control you if you should be unlucky enough to get into a permanent relationship with the owner of that body! It's natural to have sexual feelings, but if they come to dominate our lives, complications can result. Gently defusing the feelings can make us a lot more comfortable.

If you lack energy or motivation, reflect on disease and death, the way it can come at any time, or simply repeat to yourself "may I be filled with energy" over and over, while relaxing. Positive thinking, performed in a systematic way, can work wonders on the psyche. Such reflections are further explained and developed in the chapter on meditation.

4.2 Insight

There's another way.

When you understand directly what you are, when you have insight, then change comes quickly and dramatically. The difference is this: you can be told something is dangerous, but unless you see it for yourself, it doesn't always make much of an impression. My mother warned me to stay away from the hot coils of the stove, for example, and for some time I followed her advice. One day my curiosity overcame me and I touched one of the coils when it was red. I burned my finger, and never did it again.

Insight is like touching the hot stove. You really see something and understand, and you change immediately and without effort.

Unfortunately, arousing insight isn't easy. We can develop healthy habits, and in our new, healthier environment, we will become more sensitive, which in turn opens the possibility of understanding. Isn't there something more specific we can do?

That's a very difficult question to answer. If we work to change ourselves through developing healthier lifestyles, and if at the same time we put our heart and mind into observing just what's going on in and around us, insight is going to happen. Sometimes it will happen and we won't even know it. We'll understand something fundamental, but we won't realize its significance for years, when it finally clicks intellectually and we realize that we've gone through a fundamental change in the way we perceive things.

If we want a barometer, change is probably the best measure of whether or not we've truly understood or whether we've just fooled ourselves. Naturally, because insight is deemed desirable, the mind will begin working to simulate it in order to satisfy its craving for greater self-esteem. If we have a sudden flash of understanding, however, and subsequently find that certain negative behavior patterns have dropped away with little effort or conflict, then it is likely we have experienced true insight and that our mind has subsequently undergone a certain reorganization as a result.

Here's an example. Many people have a strong aversion to losing and act out when a game doesn't go their way. Suppose one such person, a tennis player, has a bad temper, throwing his racket and getting angry every time he loses a point while playing tennis. Now, why should the simple fact of losing a point create a state of internal conflict? It's simple: a highly competitive player wants to win and creates an image of himself as a winner. Bad shots are not part of that image. When the reality conflicts with the image, the player becomes angry.

If the tennis player had a true insight into this mechanism, seeing that the conflict is entirely self-fabricated, then the behavior would stop immediately upon the realization of the insight. It wouldn't be necessary to suppress his anger or redirect it, or to train himself out of it. The negative reaction would just disappear.

Insight, however, isn't how such minor behavior problems are usually treated. Instead, the player's coach might suggest that losing cool on the court is bad for his game. The player might train himself to take a few deep breaths and count to ten, or learn to channel his fury into energy of motion on the court. Other players may simply get used to the situation and stop seeing it as threatening. These are positive solutions, but are the result of rationalization and behavior modification rather than insight. While so-called self control, when all else fails, is certainly not a bad idea (in fact, I recommend it), the need for control of negative behavior indicates a shortfall of insight.

So the rule of thumb is, strong, true insight results in positive life changes that seem to require little effort. When insight is absent, life changes might be made, but usually it's more difficult, with a lot of inner conflict. After all, why stop doing what comes naturally if we don't see the danger?

On the other hand, if we truly *do* see danger, such as a cobra coiling to strike, or a wave of bombers heading our direction, we tend to take immediate action without inner conflict.

The difference between rampaging cannibals, the danger of which we can clearly see, and dangers inherent in our everyday habits and feelings, is that cannibals are a clear and present danger while lighting a cigarette or compulsively eating heavy, calorie-laden food is rather subtle. We don't notice the danger until it's too late.

That's why sensitivity is important. Here, we're not talking about the kind of sensitivity where, if you happen to accidentally slight someone, they tend to react defensively, or if you point out that they have a small pimple on their arm they become hopelessly embarrassed. That isn't really sensitivity at all, but rather a too-precarious self-image.

The kind of sensitivity needed is plain, straight-forward sensitivity of the body, the nerves, the sense organs. We listen with our eyes, see with our skin. What are we looking for? Nothing special. We're just looking at what's there, observing what is, consciousness, which is hard to miss. It's everywhere.

And a good way to start developing our sensitivity is by cultivating some healthy habits.

4.3 Summary

1. Habits can reduce our sensitivity, and ordinarily are rather neutral even when they are positive. (However, see 2.)

2. Creating healthy habits can result in improving our health and level of happiness.

3. Healthy habits may be cultivated by the use of imagination and self-suggestion.

4. Healthy habits will result in greater physical sensitivity and sharper perceptions and intellect.

5. Heightened physical sensitivity may result in our gaining deeper insight.

6. Deeper insight makes it easier for us to maintain and extend our regimen of healthy habits. It positively impacts our world view.

7. A new world view changes the way we interact with others, helping them to better themselves and their lives.

8. As other people better themselves and their personal environments, our world becomes a better place to live in.

Chapter 5

Ego, Pride, and Prejudice

As we develop physically from infancy, our minds and our memory are also developing. The memories and what little we understand of them create a sense of self. The self then acquires attributes that are considered desirable, although there may be no particular reason behind them other than cultural tradition. Here we consider some of the dynamics of such processes.

5.1   Ego

One of the most familiar entities in anyone's world is the ego. In fact, for most of us, the sense of self seems to be something so fundamental, so basic to our existence, that it's taken completely for granted. As a consequence we tend not to think much about it, and when we do, it's abstract speculation rather than any attempt to observe and find out for ourselves.

What's interesting about ego is that we often talk about it as if it were a concrete object, even when we don't really have any idea what it is. Ego is usually identified as a general feeling of self that we carry around with us as we go about our daily business. Early on we learn that we must defend and protect this sense of self, and we do so with a vengeance, often causing complications for ourselves and everyone around us.

As children we learn early on to identify ourselves with our bodies and feelings. As we grow older we begin to identify with our parents, siblings, toys, our possessions, our physical and cultural environment. We create an identity around the things and people we like. or are simply used to. As we move through childhood to young adulthood, the intellect comes more into play, and we identify ourselves with various abstract notions. "I'm an American." Or "I'm a Protestant." Many of these ideas and ideologies were planted in us when we were children, and later in life they can return to us some of the feelings of our youth, stimulated by memory, like Proust's little Madelaines and remembrances of things past.

A typical case in point is religion. Most people believe strongly in giving their children a religious education. As children, we don't have much say in the matter, so we dutifully attend Sunday School and go through the motions. Later, as teens, the years of rebellion may lead us to reject our parents' religion.

Yet suddenly the mind may give up its rebelliousness and embrace its conditioning. This surrender will naturally result in a tremendously good feeling, because at last a buried conflict is resolved once and for all. Although the tenets of the religion may not be completely reasonable, it is nonetheless very reassuring to believe them. The pure, uncomplicated sensations of youth return, to a great extent the conflict between reason and our conditioning is arrested, and all around it appears to be a win-win situation.

So on we go, spending our lives trying to define what it is we are, and it's always in terms of something else. Many of us probably remember having innumerable conversations centering around identity when we were teenagers. Identifying with someone or something is considered very important regardless of age, and when successful identification is achieved, there is the satisfying feeling of being one step closer to having an identity, to knowing ourselves. And when that thing or idea or person we identified ourselves with is attacked, we feel uncomfortable and threatened, so we strike back.

Suppose you're of French extraction and quite proud of the fact. If someone says something disparaging about the French, you might feel you have to disagree, to defend the French against this insult, because you consider yourself to be one of them.

That's how pride steps in. We identify ourselves with certain people, objects, or ideas, and then we're pleased with the fact that these people, objects, or ideas are on our side, somehow extensions of ourselves, defining what and who we are. They seem larger than we are, and it makes us feel larger to believe in them. The ideas even trigger subtle pleasurable responses in us. Eventually we have an image of who we are, based on all this identifying and imitating. The reality is usually considerably different.

Sometimes these images result in amusing or even tragic consequences. Cigarette commercials, for example, often try to create the image that a smoker is somehow more attractive or competent. Smokers are portrayed as tough cowboys or business women. Subconsciously (and sometimes consciously), we admire the images and want to imitate them. Because all these images are smoking cigarettes, we're more likely to adopt the same habit and feel good about it. The reality, of course, is that by smoking we are destroying our health.

Creating and becoming attached to self-images, in general, is hazardous to our mental health and well-being. Let me give you a personal example. I teach physics and math for a living. There was a time when, if I made a mistake in class, it would really affect me. I'd get depressed about it for the rest of the day, sometimes even brooding about the incident days later.

Why was I so affected? Pride. I had an image of myself as an excellent teacher, one who made no mistakes. When I failed to live up to the image, even for a moment, I became unhappy, unable to accept the fact that I was occasionally fallible. This led to inner conflict and depression. While there is nothing so terrible about occasional depression or conflict, it's a waste of energy, and under such circumstances indicates a general misunderstanding, a confusion of an artificial construct with reality. The image I had created of the competent instructor was unnecessary, superfluous, and actually interfered on occasion with the conduct of my work.

So why are we always encouraged to "take pride in our work"? Wouldn't society fall apart if we didn't? Wouldn't the quality of work fall, bringing modern life as we know it to a halt? That is an important question. We have, on the opposite end of the spectrum from the perfectionist, people who shrug their shoulders and say "We're all going to die. It doesn't matter how hard we try or what we do." Those people have created an image, as well. They consider themselves and their actions to be of negligible importance, which is a clear indication of confusion. Just because there are billions of people in the world doesn't mean a single individual is unimportant. The individual, from a given person's point of view, is in reality a fairly important part of the whole. After all, as we look around and observe as we go about our business, there always seems to be this hunk of flesh hanging on to us. From the personal point of view, which is the only point of view we have, this hunk of flesh and collection of thoughts and memories actually occupies a fairly large piece of our landscape, as seen from inside our skin.

So discounting our personal importance is a mistake, and can lead to lower quality in our work. And in any case, if we're going to go around making images, the images might as well be positive. We and the people around us will be a lot happier and we'll get more done. And if we're ahead in our work, we'll have the leisure time to maximize our physical and mental conditioning, and perhaps arrive at some deeper understanding. As a result, everybody will be better off. So instead of sitting around wasting time and energy being wounded by our failures, we can work on constructively trying to improve ourselves.

In what way should we improve ourselves? How do we go about it?

That's easy. Read a good book. Solve a math problem. Volunteer to help somebody out. Do a crossword puzzle. Go for a walk. Simple, everyday activities can greatly increase our value to society and to ourselves. When you're sensitive to what's going on, in and around you, then you tend to work harder and better.

So we all create images about ourselves and others, and these images cause us to do all kinds of silly things. There isn't any "me", or "ego", apart from these images, these identifications, the feelings we've identified with and carry around in our memory.

Most of us spend a large amount of time working on our images. Some people even hire expensive consultants to do it for them! We add a membership here, an affiliation there, maybe a few good deeds to round things out. Then we step back and admire ourselves and tell ourselves just how wonderful we are. And, if our bodies aren't quite what we think they ought to be, we go to a plastic surgeon to get something reshaped or simply enlarged. The next time we look at ourselves in the mirror we're pleased, although we're not quite who we used to be. All this vain behavior is caused by an obsession with our self-image.

How do we free ourselves from making these images? How can we get rid of them? Those are natural questions, but they illustrate the nature of the trap, the essential conflict. Somebody just informed us that we're obsessed with our images, and we've decided that's not a good thing. Consequently, we've decided to modify ourselves by getting rid of those images. Trying to get rid of the images, of course, is just going to perpetuate the problem. Isn't that what we're already doing? There's something about ourselves we don't like, so we try to change or eliminate it.

The alternative appears to be unacceptable: we can be just what we are. What if we're on drugs? Shouldn't we be trying to change ourselves? In extreme situations, it's important to take action. That may seem contradictory, but it's only sensible. It's comparable to what a doctor does with a very seriously ill patient, treating symptoms so the patient can become healthy enough to undergo an operation that addresses the real problem.

To free ourselves of our tendency to make and cling to images, we've got to observe them as they are. There isn't any point in suppressing them; they're still there, and we've just succeeded in hiding them from ourselves. Those images and our feelings regarding them are part of what we are. They're us. We don't want to get rid of them, we want to understand them, and we can't understand them if we refuse to look. Only through understanding can freedom be won.

5.2   Prejudice: The Alienation Effect

Prejudice is a concept that most people imagine they understand. In fact, there's much more to it than simply hating the color of someone's skin. For the liberal minded, there's a tendency to believe blindly that prejudice is always bad. What does prejudice mean, and in what sense is it ill-advised?

Prejudice means judging something or someone in advance of clear evidence. In regards prejudice against a certain person, that means assigning attributes to that person before you've allowed the person a chance to prove himself. The assigned attributes may be positive or negative. When the assigned attributes are negative, the risk is that of being grossly unfair to someone. When the assigned attributes are positive, it could mean you mislead yourself and enter into situations unfair to you.

As a matter of fact, a certain amount of prejudice is necessary to function effectively in daily life.

Suppose, for example, that every time you go to a certain restaurant you come home and are violently ill. After one or two incidents of that nature, you're not likely to go back to that restaurant. Yet that's prejudice: simply because it was bad before doesn't mean it's going to be bad the next time. Further, it may be your illnesses are coincidental. A couple of bad experiences, which may not be the restaurant's fault at all, can lead to a kind of prejudice.

Here's another example of prejudice. Suppose it's known that in a certain neighborhood street gangs regularly commit crimes against citizens. Suppose you're walking along a dark street at night in that neighborhood and you see a possible member of a gang walking toward you carrying a machete. It would be prudent to cross to the other side of the street, or maybe break into a run, yet that's prejudice. You've seen somebody and assumed that he's dangerous when in fact he may be completely innocent, and is brandishing that bloody machete just for exercise. So this is prejudice, too, but there is no need to be fair-minded to the point of losing your common sense.

How do we know when prejudice is justified? Most of the time you can tell by how you feel. Generally, unreasonable prejudice is something that you feel righteous about, something that makes you feel powerful and strong in a hateful or angry way, or more pleasurably alive. When the state of prejudice begins, you will usually notice the defenses kicking in at the same time, justifying your prejudice so you can feel good about it.

Another kind of prejudice involves a sense of rectitude. Why do we always have to be right? What does it matter if we're wrong once in a while? We must be right because we're afraid to be wrong. We identify so much with our ideas and opinions that we feel personally attacked when someone says those opinions are not correct. Therefore we must defend them. Images again, getting tangled up with reality.

Now, how can we get rid of prejudice? That's a natural question, but it implies we're still trying to modify our behavior rather than understand it. In the end we've got to understand the root of prejudice in order to be free of it. Prejudice has a number of roots: lack of information, misinformation, fear, or habit. We identify with certain ideas, practices, places, and languages, things we're used to, and people who are different from us are automatically assumed to pose a threat. Sometimes they really are a threat, of course, but most of the time the differences between people are very slight.

Understanding prejudice takes sensitivity. We've also got to be courageous, willing to take a chance on being wrong once in a while. The key is world view. Once the world is seen as whole, complete, in its totality, it's more difficult for prejudices to remain rooted. And when our personality assumes its true proportion, we stop having to be right all the time. Truth becomes more important than opinion. What does it matter who's right? We are part of the whole, and so is that other person, and our interest is not what is just good for us, but what is best for everyone.

Chapter 6

Love

One of the most important and misunderstood words in any language is the word for love. What is love? Are there different kinds of love? How do we know when it's real? In this chapter the meaning of love will be explored. As might be expected, it's a complex subject, wrapped up in the demands associated with species survival.

6.1   Parental Love of Children

Humankind is endowed with a fabulous information system that goes by the code letters DNA, short for deoxyribonucleic acid. Starting from a single fertilized cell that would fit easily on the head of a pin, DNA develops and controls that miraculous creature called a human being. Without our conscious effort, billions of cells in our body go about their daily activities, partly directed by neural and hormonal impulses. We breathe automatically, even when asleep. Our hearts keeps beating. Our stomachs break food down and our intestines gather the nutrients into the blood stream, where they are distributed and utilized. And all of these processes and more function together with a competence and precision that is nothing short of miraculous. The amazing complexity of this control makes even the most untalented person among us something special.

Given the incredible abilities of our DNA, it should come as no surprise that we have natural mechanisms responsible for ensuring our survival and continuance as a species. Many of these natural mechanisms are identified as somehow connected to the concept of love.

When my daughter was only a year and a half old it was already clear that she had a special attraction to objects smaller than herself, particularly if the object looked like a miniature person. By the time she was two and a half she had a very strongly developed sense of what mothering was all about and was very interested in acting out the care and feeding of a baby. This was a great revelation to me: it dawned on me over a period of some months that there is a natural tendency to consider miniature objects, both human and otherwise, to be special and attractive. That's partly why people like model trains and planes, and why children love to play with dolls. Nature has endowed us with an instinctual perception that causes us to view miniatures as pleasing.

The reason for this tendency is obvious. Babies and young children are miniature adults. The pleasure derived in viewing miniature people helps us develop caring families where children are protected and nurtured. Mother love is especially strong, as it must and should be. This kind of love is instinctual, and it's very advantageous, in every way, to have strong protective instincts. Sometimes this type of love translates to others of adult size, especially grown children.

I have noticed that when regarding another person while in this instinctive mode, the person often appears physically smaller. The brain resizes the perception to match the instinct. And the opposite can be true: a smaller authority figure can appear larger.

Now, while mother love and similar protective impulses are highly desirable traits, there is some question whether or not we can truly call it "love". Love is supposed to be unconditional, isn't it? Could we feel that same kind of love towards someone who had done grievous injury to our family or other loved ones? That would be a considerable challenge. It follows that instinctive parental love is not absolute and unconditional.

6.2   Attachment

There is another kind of love which is emotional in nature, and is basically a kind of programming of the mind and nervous system. This kind of love happens when someone spends a lot of time with you, and you do things together. It's bonding based on culture: people gesture similarly, eat similar foods, help each other, talk the same way, share experiences, like the same games and holidays and so forth. To a certain extent these feelings may be hard-wired: a tendency to band together with others of like disposition and characteristics, and to encourage bonding by imitating others has positive social benefits. This kind of bonding also happens in families and is something like a comfortable habit. You're used to having someone around, so when that person isn't around you feel something's missing. You get lonely. And because you are lonely and incomplete without that person, you might say you love that person.

This kind of love could be called attachment. Evidently it's not absolute and unconditional. We become attached to all kinds of people and things, even when those people sometimes abuse us. There are two roots to this: habit and fear. Habits are easy, and when things are going well enough we're afraid to change. Deep inside we're terribly lonely, and the constant companionship of certain people or things is reassuring. In addition, such attachments are valuable in establishing a community network, which is highly advantageous in terms of survival.

The mechanism of attachment became clear to me when I went for a several-week meditation retreat at Live Oak Island, a small Florida community on

Appalachicola Bay. I stayed in a big empty house owned by my aunt and uncle while they were on vacation. Virtually no one else lived on the island, at least not on a full time basis. After a few days of seeing no one at all I began to feel lonely and a little scared. It was uncomfortable being all by myself, silent and isolated, especially at night.

Then one day, all of a sudden, I realized I wasn't alone. I had the grass, the spiders and insects, the birds and the trees. I had the marsh, the gulf, the Sun and the Moon. I wasn't lonely or afraid anymore, and since that time I've experienced the sensation of loneliness only for short periods of time, for an hour here or there, such as when I moved from Florida to Arizona, leaving my family behind while I set up a home for them there. Loneliness is a transient sensation based on a particular world view. Getting all worried about it just magnifies and prolongs the discomfort.

As far as my brother-Sun, sister-Moon perception goes, I don't take it too seriously. I saw that attachments to the environment can supplant attachments to human beings. I wouldn't call it a terribly deep insight on the nature of consciousness. My perception at that time was dualistic, because I viewed the Sun, Moon, and so forth as separate and distinct from my inner world. At best there was a glimmer of a new world view, no more.

Attachment, by the way, has been unfairly criticized in certain religions. We're advised to be detached from worldly things, our spouses, our cars, our possessions. When we try to be detached, all that happens is that we become less sensitive, which leads to complications in our relationships. Rather than try to create some simulation of somebody we aren't, it's more productive to perceive what we are. Our suffering from attachments or loneliness is far more interesting than attempts to fake ourselves out with manufactured feelings. Direct perception of what we are can precipitate spontaneous understanding and action.

6.3   Romance

Aside from instinctual love for our children and tribal love for our clan, there is romantic, or sexual love. Taking care of our children is extremely important, but it's rather futile unless we've got some to take care of in the first place. To this end, nature equipped us with sex organs and arranged the hormones and sensations in such a way that we sometimes get obsessed by them. This obsession is the phenomenon of falling in love.

Falling in love is conditional because it has as its object a particular person. It's based on the person's sexual attractiveness. It's no coincidence that the object of desire often has some of the same characteristics of one or both of the parents of the romantically-obsessed person.

Romantic obsession is characterized by a compulsion to think about a particular person constantly. Sleep and work are interrupted by these compulsive thoughts. When the feeling isn't mutual, then life can become difficult for the obsessed individual. That single other person seems to be enormously important, and that overblown perception of importance can lead to all the crazy things that people do when they're in love. To a large extent they can't help themselves: they're programmed to procreate with those having certain fairly obvious characteristics, with similar culture and personality, and running into someone having those attributes sets off hormonal and neural activity that are virtually irresistible. And those feelings are considerably magnified when the focal person responds in a positive way.

Ordinary, everyday lust is the garden variety of sexual obsession. It's based on reactions to superficial stimuli, and can arise frequently throughout the day. I recall a study where it was found that the average male thinks of sex once every few minutes. The difference between lust and sexual obsession is that lust doesn't stick. The eye roves on and the stimulus is forgotten. In sexual obsession, the mind keeps reviewing the chosen stimuli, over and over again, fanning the flames of desire. That creates a drunken condition of mind which is highly pleasurable, and which is induced by various hormones and neurotransmitters, particularly for the purpose of inducing a powerful bond with a person of the opposite (usually) sex.

While it's great to be in love and have that love returned, it certainly can be hazardous to our long-term welfare and happiness. Many people enter into marriage or other sexual relationships too readily, eager to consummate the relationship, convinced by their hormones, their hard-wiring and their conditioning that they've found the one and only person who can remove their feelings of separateness once and for all.

Naturally this is not the case, as the high divorce rate makes clear. The problem is that after the honeymoon is over and sexual appetites have been satiated, the lovers only then start to really get to know each other. Prior to that, they've been courting and on their best behavior. With the demands of hormones reduced and the excitement of novelty worn off, the two spouses are confronted with the reality of the person they've elected to spend the rest of their lives with. Sometimes they are disappointed.

Many people manage to cope with the disparities that become apparent only after the marriage knot is tied. However a lot of pain and suffering must be born by those less successful, especially when children are involved.

So how do we handle sexual obsession when it occurs? How do we know if it's for real? Well, in one sense, it's always for real–fueled by delusion, perhaps, but delusion is real, too. And emotional difficulties are great training grounds. Without hurdles, why jump?

That isn't to say that embroiling ourselves in difficult relationships is a good idea. On the contrary, we have enough personal problems without deliberately generating more of them. But it's also true that in order to learn, certain risks must be taken. Hiding from complications will prevent us from realizing our full potential as human beings, and that potential is considerable.

Whether you are male or female, you're going to be facing strong sexual feelings sooner or later. Cold showers might help a little. You also would probably not want sexual tensions to build to enormous peaks without some healthy release. In most cultures, too much is made of the transient, albeit intense pleasures of sex, and given the repercussions of irresponsible sexual behavior, that isn't surprising. But sex is a natural part of our makeup, like breathing or any other function, and in itself isn't inconsistent with spirituality. In some traditions, such as the tantric tradition, sexuality is even used as a vehicle to deeper spiritual understanding.

Something that might be valuable in combatting sexual obsession is reflecting on the factual attributes of the physical body. Sit quietly in your room at night, imagining the various parts of your body in turn, as if reviewing for an anatomy exam. Think about the blood coursing through your body, your bones, teeth, the underlying connective tissue, the excretory system. Think also about how the body is subject to decay. The person you're obsessed with today will be worn out in a few years, just as you will be. Do you really want to base your relationship mainly on physical appearance? It won't last forever.

The physical side, of course, is only part of the picture. There are all the other resonances, springing from the images you stored of your parents and their relationship when you were very young. And there is the image you have of the other person, built up from the common experiences, the way they think, dress, talk, and generally behave. So whereas much of the above discussion on sexual obsession focuses on the physical, there are also powerful emotional and psychological forces. Not satisfied with a unidimensional attack, DNA, in conjunction with evolution, has created a whole collection of different routes to the goal of reproduction.

Another good mechanism for reducing obsession is yoga. Obsession wires you tight, yoga softens you, relaxes you, and clarifies your mind. The full lotus pose and head stand are especially effective, if you can manage them safely and comfortably.

So it's important to keep things in perspective even when your head is spinning around like crazy. This holds especially true after marriage: obsession can strike again, and cause serious marital disruption.

6.4 Habitual Love

A more mature love, as it is sometimes called, often develops after the sex wears off. This kind of relating is based on growing friendship, mutual cooperation, shared memories, and habit. Marriage after the development of friendship is usually more reliable than one based on sexual obsession.

As valuable as is mature love in a long-lasting relationship, this love is again generally conditional. Many marriages end because of infidelity: obviously, in these cases, fidelity is a precondition of such relationships. We expect our partners to behave in certain ways, and when they deviate too much or too often, we find it difficult to love them. Some will argue that they still love their spouse, it's just the spouse's behavior that they don't like. Our behavior, however, is part of what we are, and a love conditioned on behavior is a social contract that is mutually beneficial and laudable, but not the kind of love we're talking about when we speak of, for example, Jesus and his love for us.

Like the other varieties of love, habitual love has its place in a well-functioning home. Children need stability, and a general feeling of bonding helps keep the family together during times of stress. It's sensible, it's just not what love really is. True love is something far beyond peaceful coexistence.

6.5   Unconditional Love

We've discussed instinctual love, habitual love, obsessions, and social contracts, and I think we're probably agreed that while these are powerful and often highly meritorious or useful, they aren't really absolute in any sense. What is absolute love? Love that is not conditional? Is it possible, or is it just an unattainable ideal?

First of all, if such love exists, you can't make it. If you could, it would depend on the process. You also can't preserve it in any way. You can't practice it.

On the face of it, this sounds impossible. Everything else in life we gained through training, practice of some kind or another, trial and error. But there is, in fact, a tremendous potential for love in each and every person. Unfortunately, this potential is chained up, blocked. And although it's in each of us and is perfectly natural, no act of force or compulsion, regardless of how subtle, can cause it to express itself. The barrier we've erected is too tall and strong. What is this formidable barrier to love?

We are.

That's right. The world view that we are separate from everything and everybody. The biasing of our perception by this world view.

When we see that this separation is arbitrary, a transformation takes place. When there is no dividing of the world into inside and outside, we understand what love is. It's something that's powerful and deep, steady and strong. When there is no separation between our self and universe, all adversaries vanish.

Unconditional love is impossible while the delusion of duality holds sway. Only when the delusion is set aside can love come into being. Absolute love is unconditional because it isn't based on anything, but on the absence of something. When dualistic perception stops, for whatever reason, love is what remains.

6.6   Awakening to Love

Love is so important that discovering it shouldn't be left to chance. There are two main routes to awakening to love, one of them essentially the development of habit as discussed in a previous chapter, and the other a byproduct of the development of insight. Awakening love through habit sounds contradictory, but it's highly beneficial to lay down pathways of access in the mind through self-improvement activities. The direct development of insight, on the other hand, is generally more difficult.

6.6.1 Love by Suggestion

The human mind is open to suggestion. Ordinarily nothing is systematically suggested, so the general experiences of everyday life gets stored there, gradually conditioning our responses and world view. Instead of this laissez-faire, we can proactively create desirable mental states through suggestion.

The fundamental technique is reflection. You sit down quietly, back straight, and begin wishing yourself happiness repeatedly as if drilling a mantra. For example, you could think "May I be free from anger and disease, may no harm come to me, may I be happy", or some such, imagining this state as you do so. Starting with yourself is essential: hatred often is the result of inner conflicts and frustrations, and it's important to first like yourself, as you are. After your positive feelings towards yourself are firmly established, it then makes sense to spread those positive feelings out to include others.

It is interesting that although absolute love is unconditional, you can create a simulation of it by exercises of this sort. What's happening here is simple: your old habits of thought are being displaced by new habits of thought, and these particular habits are conducive to a kinder, gentler view of the world. And because your simulation is also conducive to greater composure and calm, you're more likely to develop true insight, which in turn opens you up to love.

Many people confuse absolute love with an imitation of a door mat. "Turn the other cheek" has received such wonderful press that many are confused in situations demanding action. Turning cheek is a good practice most of the time, and can lead to a calming of the mind, an opening of the heart. Sometimes, however, compassion also requires action. When someone injures you, the correct action might be to turn the other cheek. Other times it may be better, in the grand scheme of things, to hit that person back. After all, you've got to help him learn that such aggressive behavior will sooner or later lead to trouble.

So if you see a poisonous snake, and it represents a threat to you or your family, you take action. I once killed a coral snake that was entering my garage. I didn't like having to do it, and it occurred to me that I could try capturing it and releasing it safely in the forest, but there was deadly risk involved. So I murmured an apology and hit it with a rake.

I felt no malice towards the snake, but I don't think that made the snake feel much better.

In daily life there usually isn't much call for physical violence, but there are numerous analogous situations, such as when someone insults or slights you, or makes disparaging comments of a friend or of some group of people. Sometimes it's best to remain silent. Other times it's absolutely necessary to speak, although you risk an argument and a lot of trouble. It's also possible that with very difficult people there's nothing you can do except stay out of their way. Right action takes good judgement, and good judgement requires a clear mind, unfettered by prejudice of any kind.

It's useful, by the way, to remember that those who challenge or otherwise annoy us are very useful to us, because by our spontaneous reactions we might uncover ourselves, our true feelings, our true nature.

6.6.2   Love through Insight

Unconditional love is something I had not the slightest understanding of before December of 1991, shortly after my fortieth birthday, when, in the span of a few seconds, the foundation of the greater part of this book became clear to me. And it took insight, powerful insight, to see, to understand, to experience love for the first time in my life. The insight was non-verbal; rather, it was perceptual and instantaneous.

Imagine looking at someone and seeing no separation between that person and you, not in terms of the imagination, but in reality, simply, directly. Imagine going about your daily business, utterly convinced, because you observe it directly, that you, your personality, is nothing more than a fragment of the whole, and that whole is not something abstract or removed but in fact is everything you experience, everything you are.

Once you see that, actually with your mind, heart, your nerves, your entire being, then negative feelings like hatred, lust, envy, and jealousy are dramatically weakened. You may still experience such feelings, but because your personality is at the proper magnification, neither too big nor too small in your world view but just the right size, the feelings are brief and muted, they don't lead to obsessions that create further problems. It is possible that with sufficiently deep insight, negative feelings actually cease altogether, although at present I can only speculate.

Words are inadequate to certain tasks. What I'm doing here is pointing out what I see and how I see it, describing my view of the world to the best of my current ability. The description is only a crude indicator of something that is as subtle as a knife thrust to the belly when you first really see it. The first good look makes a powerful and lasting impression. It led to my writing this book.

I assert that it is possible to love in the absolute sense and that anyone is fundamentally capable of it. That said, a common question is to ask whether it's possible to love like that all the time. The question is meaningless. Either you love or you don't, you can't arouse it at will, because what you then have is a simulation, you're just faking it. Love happens when the habit of dividing the world into self and other takes a rest. It's spontaneous and natural, and will arise when you are released from the chains of your own memory.

The past is memory, and it has been proven scientifically that memory can significantly influence perception. In familiar surroundings our memories puts a filter over everything, muting the intensity and immediateness of our experience. When by vigilant observation we observe that happening, something miraculous occurs: the interference caused by memory ceases. Our perceptions become fresh, as when we were children, and we feel an immediate and powerful contact with all the phenomena in our experience.

That freedom from the past is love, a total, unconditional love that is powerful and strong. In the light of that love there is no division. A noisy muffler is like beautiful music, miraculous and rich, while the waves on the river ripple through your extended body and the birds fly through a sky without boundaries and with no beyond. That's the unconditional love that arises when, by grace or chance or powerful insight, the shackles of the past fall away.

Chapter 7

Dealing with Unhappiness

Why are we unhappy? Why can't we be happy all the time? Why do other people always seem to be happier than we are?

Some of you may feel like you're already happy. Why? Well, for one thing, it's very likely everything is going your way. You're not sick, you've got a nice car, some money in the bank, and maybe a spouse you get along with and some great kids. You've got everything.

On the other hand, it doesn't take much to make a person perfectly miserable. Everything else can be going right, but one little thing can spoil it all. A blemish, a rejection letter, a low grade in a course, a negative performance review, a tactless comment. These are a few of the many things that can send us unexpectedly into a depression.

A root cause of a lot of unhappiness is comparison. Most people in the world, for example, occupy what are essentially dead end jobs. That's just a fact of life, not something to be unhappy about. But we compare ourselves to someone who is more successful, and we start to get depressed and unhappy.

What's even more interesting is that the better off we are, the less it takes to make us unhappy. I've known people who had lots of money, good health, talent, and good looks, and yet the smallest things could send them spiraling into depression, or make them angry or annoyed. We have a tendency to take for granted what we've already got, and to focus on whatever isn't right. When too much is going right, then the small reverses that ordinarily wouldn't merit much attention get magnified out of proportion. We compare what we have to what we would like to have, and of course, what we don't have is always much better.

So comparison, in general, is a good way to create a state of unhappiness. We might see someone who is extremely attractive physically, for example, then reflect upon our own body and start to feel inadequate. We focus on what's wrong, forgetting everything that's right.

And we are truly amazing: just the fact we can think and function and move around is a miracle in itself. Imagine trillions of individual cells acting in concert!

Another common reaction having its roots in comparison is competitiveness. We compete with others to beat them and feel good about ourselves. While this is a good step or two up from being depressed and down on our luck, it still isn't a very healthy outlook in the broad view of things. A certain amount of competitiveness can be fun, and is not necessarily bad as long as everyone realizes it's just a game. When the wrong kind of competitiveness takes hold of a person, however, the victim can get overworked, testy, easily angered, and generally unpleasant to be around. A ruthlessness develops that feeds on itself, enlarging the ego with each and every victory, no matter how inconsequential. Pretty soon they're beating their kids at games and taking great pleasure in it.

There are various cures for the kind of unhappiness caused by comparison. Some of the cures are reasonably positive and healthy, while others are marginal or negative. Most people escape their unhappiness by resorting to distracting sensations like food, sex, or TV. Others escape into competitions. Escaping our problems with diversions doesn't do anything to resolve them. Unless our problems are addressed and resolved through understanding, we'll be forced to continue escaping from them in a continuous cycle of fear and evasion.

Other things can cause general unhappiness and depression, such as diet and physical condition, but often the problem is rooted in comparison and a desire to suppress, repress, or otherwise escape reality. Failing exams, getting fired from a job, being treated unjustly, dealing with serious health problems, being abused by someone–all the normal, everyday problems that people have to put up with, can cause unhappiness. Such reasons for the onset of unhappiness are considered 'valid', but whether our unhappiness is valid or not is really unimportant. What matters is recognizing when we're unhappy and developing strategies to handle it. These strategies fall into three main categories, which we'll discuss in turn: the Pollyanna Principle, Positive Thinking, and Insight.

7.1   The Pollyanna Principle

The Pollyanna Principle is a common method of dealing with unhappiness and can be a valuable tool. It's also a part of our culture, and has been passed down through the ages. The main advantage is the simplicity: "count your blessings". Most of us have been so admonished numerous times, especially by our mothers.

And it's very sound advice. Think of all the things you've got going for you, and of all the people less fortunate. Get your life into perspective and you'll start to feel better. This is a time-honored tool of feelings management. It can be compared to a kind of mental judo, because often comparison got you down in the first place, and to get back up, you compare yourself to those worse off than you, rather than with those more fortunate. And you realize that the hand you were dealt might not be so bad after all.

For example, suppose you lose your job. That's clearly bad news, but you can always reflect that there are those with serious medical conditions, such as blindness, who can never even hope to have a job like yours. If you're down to your last dollar, you can think of those who are forced to dig through trash cans to find half-eaten food. It's very rare than anyone has such bad luck that it isn't possible to find an example of somebody even worse off.

So by reflecting on those who are less fortunate, we can take the sting out of our personal situation. We're not alone; everyone has problems, and some of them have more problems than we do.

7.2 Positive Thinking

Positive thinking may appear to be much the same as practicing the Pollyanna Principle, to which it's related, but in fact it's far more powerful. The idea is to create a positive mental state by reflecting on certain positive images or thoughts. Negative habits of thought can lead to a pretty gloomy outlook. Certain patterns of negative thinking lend themselves to the creation of unpleasant mental states, which in turn means you're not going to be a very happy person.

So one answer is to deliberately supplant the negative thoughts with positive thoughts. You'll be amazed at how much better you feel. Fast relief!

Here's something I've done which is effective. It's actually a meditation technique, and is discussed further in the chapter on meditation. Sit quietly in a room or under a tree, relax, and think, over and over, "may I be happy". Just keep it going in your mind, over and over, while you relax. Sounds easy, doesn't it? It is. Another favorite of mine, a bit longer, is "May I be free of anger and disease, may no harm come to me, may I take care of myself happily". Envision yourself taking good care of yourself, being healthy and safe. Believe it or not, negative thinking can spoil your mood. This little exercise displaces the negative thoughts with positive ones.

Note that you're not saying "I'm happy, I'm happy, I'm happy!" Such a practice would not work well at all, because the phrase itself indicates a desire to avoid reality: that is, the reality that you are unhappy. You'll start to feel a certain strain, because what you're thinking is contrary to the reality, and you will therefore be in a state of conflict. Wishing happiness on yourself, on the other hand, does not entail denying reality. That's important, because the root cause of depression is the desire to avoid reality. So instead you say "may I" be happy. Just wish yourself well. Major and minor reversals in our lives can make us dislike or even hate ourselves, and that can, in turn, cause us to hate others. So this practice is useful in promoting our mental health.

Now, you may be thinking it's self-centered to sit around wishing yourself happiness. Weren't we taught that such self-preoccupation is egotistical, narrow, and selfish? On the contrary: nothing could be further from the truth. Self-love has been given a bad rap since ancient times. The simple fact of the matter is that while other people are indeed important, so indeed are you. You're a person just like they are, aren't you? And people who abuse themselves and others often do so simply because they dislike themselves, so anything that makes you feel better about yourself will make you feel better about other people. You'll find yourself helping others because you really want to, not just because someone told you it's the right thing to do.

To get back to the technique, just keep reflecting as outlined above. After a while, you'll usually start to feel much better. Somebody cares about you after all, and it's you! As you warm up to yourself, you stop taking your shortcomings so seriously. After all, if your best friend had messed up like you did, you'd just shrug it off, wouldn't you?

Now, after you feel pretty good about yourself, you can extend the same thoughts toward a close friend, then relatives, then everyone else, gradually expanding to include everything and everybody, in all directions and all ways. Just use the same basic formula, wishing happiness on others. It's not a bad idea to carry this mantra around with you all day.

We're so used to feeling down or depressed when we fail that it seems completely natural. In fact, something more subtle is going on. We had an image of ourselves as competent and successful, and when that image is at odds with reality we become depressed mainly because we're trying to deny that reality. Consider the kinds of thoughts that go through a person's mind after a failure of some kind: "I shouldn't have done this", or "If only I had done that." All the regrets for actions that, at the time, were the best we could muster. That's a sure sign of the struggle between the image and the reality.

Similar activity surrounds nearly any unwanted experience, whether your own or that of someone close to you. On the one hand there is the image of what the world "ought to be", and on the other the painful reality. Creating this schism takes a lot of energy. So much so that you don't have too much energy left over for getting around. That's why you feel physically depressed. Weak. Run down. Like you could sink into the ground and save everybody the cost of a burial. And this brings us to the next method for coping with depression and general unhappiness, the most powerful by far.

7.3   Insight

The reason insight is so powerful is because it goes to the root of the problem and eliminates it.

Unfortunately, it is also the most difficult technique to apply because we're used to dealing with the universe dualistically, us and them, inside and outside, with us on the inside and them on the outside. The first two methods essentially involve the use of the dualistic point of view in a clever way, to trick and program the mind into a more positive state. Call it mental judo. With insight, by contrast, the root problem is perceived directly, and the result is liberation.

The root of the problem is the rejection of reality, clinging to an image of how we think our life ought to be and an obsession with whatever is imperfect, along with an overwhelming desire that it not be so. Seeing this, truly and not just intellectually, will result in instant, long- lasting relief. And while it's difficult in practice, it's easy in principle. Here's the long and short of it: sit quietly and observe the sensations, bad and good, as they arise.

Then what? Then nothing. Just keep watching them. Don't watch TV, don't raid the refrigerator, don't bother your spouse. Besides, you're probably depressed because of some major problem in your relationship anyway, and your spouse wouldn't touch you with a rubber- sheathed ten foot pole.

Just hang out with that very interesting feeling of depression. Make friends with it. Get to know it.

It might be thought that this technique is abstract or speculative, but it's based on my personal direct experience. Once, some years ago, I was depressed about a relationship, so much so that I didn't feel like moving around too much. Many people deal with such problems either by wallowing in them or by trying to distract themselves from them, and of course I have dealt with such problems that way, as well. This time, however, I sat there and simply watched the feeling. I didn't turn on a radio, I didn't try to somehow distract myself from the feeling. I just watched it.

After watching a while, I realized that I was perceiving the feeling of depression, which seemed enormous, as being at a certain spatial location. The room was only dimly lit, and the sensation of depression appeared to be approximately five or six inches away from "me". In other words, the place I identified as myself, that place a few inches behind the eyes, and the feeling of depression were separated in space, with the sensation I identified as me behind my eyes and the sensation of depression as somewhere outside of me.

What was going on? Mentally, I had taken the feelings and rejected them, pushed them away. My mind began calling that complex of sensations constituting the depression "not-me", and therefore began to perceive it as separate and distinct from "me". I had constructed a sense of separation, of distance, between the two sensations.

While I watched this localized patch of unpleasant feelings, I gradually began to realize that those feelings were part of me. I kept watching, and after a while, the feelings didn't seem so threatening anymore. Incredibly, I was warming up to them!

As I began to lose my fear of those feelings, an interesting thing began to happen. The perceived distance between what I considered to be me and the unpleasant sensations began shrinking as I watched. It eased down to about four inches, then three, then two.

Suddenly the distance reduced to zero, and I made contact with those feelings of depression. At that instant the feelings seemed to burst like a water balloon, and I was filled with energy and happiness.

How can this experience be explained? I was using an enormous amount of energy just maintaining that illusion of distance between "me" and the unpleasant sensations. When I relaxed and simply observed without trying to change anything, I was able to see that there wasn't really a threat. The tension, the fear, began to ease, and when contact was made, all that pent up energy was released.

I dealt with depression several times in this fashion, and now for some years appear to be largely free of that mental state. The key is to relax and try not to do anything except to observe it. Sitting up is best, because lying down you might fall asleep and accidentally miss out on clearing up the problem. After you have some practice with this technique, you'll find that you rarely ever get down. Every time you meet it with calm observation, you weaken that tendency until you finally eliminate it.

So now we have three techniques. I frankly don't know how easy it would be for anyone to implement that last technique, so it's probably best to rely on the first two. The Pollyanna Principle is always pretty good, and if that doesn't work, Positive Thinking can be deployed. Using the insight method takes some courage and a certain clarity of mind that many may have forgotten, although it's probably our most natural state of being. Most of us will sit there and look at the unpleasant feelings, all the while wondering when they're going to go away. That kind of attitude, which is difficult to avoid, actually prevents the healing process.

So the creation of images, the expectations, the anticipations, are all setting us up for a fall. Truly understanding this through direct perception will bring fast relief to anyone suffering from virtually any depression, quickly restoring a sense of well-being. It's important to remember, however, that depression and unhappiness are sometimes caused by physical conditions outside of our control. The cause could be dietary, or poor physical conditioning, or from some subtle disease. So for very strong or persistent bouts of unhappiness it is advisable to consult a physician or other health professional.

Now, what do you do if you're perfectly healthy and simply can't make any progress at all on getting over your depression? What if you think the situation is getting out of hand? By all means, seek temporary relief. While escaping into food, sex, or other stimuli is not going to solve your problems, it's not necessarily a bad idea to let yourself go once in a while, as long as you don't overdo it. Dull the sensations a little, make them more manageable. There's no need to be fanatical about insight, after all. Just remember, the way life works, there will be plenty of other opportunities. So if this time around you just can't tolerate sitting there and watching those unpleasant feelings, turn on the TV or indulge in some other low-key escape. Or call a friend and talk it over. Talking your problems over with someone else opens you up, and when you start to open you're that much closer to making contact with what's bothering you, with breaking the pattern of rejection. Or you might take a jog, get your blood moving so your mind can function clearly. Do something! It's not just your problem, it's you, and you might as well get to work on it, using any tool at your disposal.

Chapter 8

Varieties of Religious Experience

Religious experience is central to the lives of most people. Even those who reject religion often value religious tenets. When discussing religious experience, problems in communication arise due to cultural contexts and differences. Ideally, then, we would like to distill and purify the essential religious experiences.

None of what you will read here is theoretical or speculative: I will report as accurately as I can everything I understand from first-hand observation. Some of it you may find controversial or disturbing, particularly if you already have a strong opinion as to what constitutes religious experience. Please feel free to believe anything you want. Here, I can only report the truth as I see it. Believing or disbelieving me won't make much difference. Blind belief has nothing to do with truth and everything to do with self-deception.

The most common vehicle in the world for promoting the healing and general welfare of the mind is the cultivation of religious experience. As the natural reverses of life bear down on us, we start looking around for something, anything, that can help us cope. And religious experience is a powerful influence because it purports to answer all the most fundamental questions. At the same time it gives us some anchor of hope in what seems otherwise to be a chaotic and incomprehensible world.

Virtually everyone in the world has been thoroughly exposed to religious thought of one kind or another. Religion, in turn, promotes certain modifications to each person's world view. Our parents, in the vast majority of cases, subscribe to the traditional world view which cuts the universe up into a million separate pieces. They superimpose upon this world view a collection of beliefs which extends that world view to a so-called unseen or spiritual world. The world view and the religious beliefs then are supposed to cover all known and all unknown experiences, which makes for a nice, neat package.

People profess undergoing religious experiences for a number of different of reasons. In some cases these experiences give us personal validity within our society, and thus are sought after. In other words, by having a certain experience and communicating it to others, we become accepted by our fellow men and women and enjoy psychological security as a result.

The search for personal validity is symptomatic of a very interesting pattern of behavior. First, we feel we are somehow separate from others, left out of the group. They are all professing their experiences, and we aren't, and we'd like to be like them. Our comparison of them with us, with special attention to the differences, makes us feel we're lacking something. We feel alone, left out. To remove this feeling of being left out, we undergo religious rituals and profess certain religious beliefs or experiences, joining the crowd.

The irony is that all the while we are trying to remedy this feeling of separateness, we are actually making the problem worse, reaffirming our separateness, getting our egos stroked by the other members of the club that has finally admitted us. Before, when we felt alone and left out, isolated, we were actually seeing our situation clearly. But the pleasure of acceptance, of social advancement, covers up the feelings of separateness, fooling us into thinking we've solved our problem. The problem is still there; we are just pleasured out of feeling it any longer.

Blind belief is something like taking morphine to cure cancer. You'll feel better, but it won't cure you.

In the midst of our chosen groups and affiliations, we still guard a divided view of the world, of inside as opposed to outside, self and other. Our sense of separation is stronger than ever, because we've identified with a new belief system, and our qualms and fears are allayed by our new friends who are eager to recognize us, and receive recognition in return.

That kind of reasoning may seem somewhat cynical and paranoid. After all, aren't there bonafide religious experiences? Can't we directly perceive religious truth? And, when and if we do, aren't there ways we can be sure our experience is valid?

The good news is that the answer to each of those difficult questions is yes. The bad news is that it isn't easy. Let's take a closer look at the varieties of religious experiences.

8.1   The Honeymoon Effect

The first and most common religious experience derives from finding a religious group that we can identify with and subsequently joining it. Note the word "identify". We find our identity in these organizations, in their beliefs, and in the people in them. After joining up there often is a feeling of euphoria that might last for some weeks or months, even years. That euphoria is virtually the same euphoria that we may experience when we fall in love. We're accepted, we've got a network, we're enthusiastic about our group, but like love-struck puppies, we're not very critical. We tend not to think too much about what we're doing, nor try to understand what we're getting into. We accept a lot of things on faith, get socially involved with other members, learn the buzz words, and that's the beginning and end of it.

Like falling in love, adopting a belief system feels so good we don't ever want it to stop, and we're often too eager to share our good fortune with others. They, too, must feel the euphoria, particularly because we've suspended our powers of critical thinking, so convincing others becomes very important to keeping ourselves convinced. We feel threatened by those who don't think as we do, and often pray to convert them, save their souls, or otherwise get them to conform to our way of thinking. The fact of the matter is, we're mainly trying to save our own souls. We're desperate to have others agree with us so we can be assured we haven't made a mistake.

The conversion-euphoria comes from being socially accepted and from the considerable relief of putting aside the annoying burden of trying to understand anything for ourselves. Our life becomes significantly simplified, and that's a very positive benefit, because it can seem awfully complicated sometimes. Someone else is making the decisions, others far greater than we have gone before and blazed the path, and so forth and so on, and all we've got to do is follow them.

Such herd behavior is seductive, but it won't solve our problems or bring true understanding. Anything based on belief and imitation holds no promise of arousing insight.

While blind belief feels good, like marriages based on the dizzy, drunken state of uncritical "love", there is considerable danger of becoming complacent, trapped in static beliefs until the end of our lives. Satisfied with a solution that holds fear of the unknown at bay, we stop learning. That is not to say this suspension of disbelief and critical regard is not without benefits, but it's something like taking a tranquilizer to keep our cool. Belief gives us something to hang on to, something that helps suspend the terrifying sense of being alone and out of control in a huge and menacing universe.

But the truth is we're still trapped, far worse than when we were young and impressionable and unsure of ourselves.

Conversion experiences can vary in intensity. Some may be very emotional and moving, dramatic. That is particularly true if we've been well-conditioned when young. When we suspend the operation of our critical intelligence, the conditioning bursts forth, flooding us with the memory of the pure sensations of childhood, like Proust and his petite madelaines.

Once we've had a conversion experience, our next problem is finding out whether our experience is valid. How do we know it's real? How do we know we're not just fooling ourselves, or that some unprincipled influence with horns and pitchfork isn't taking us for a ride?

The answer is, we don't know. And, fortunately, we don't really need to know, as long as we continue to question our moment-to-moment experience, especially in regards so-called religious experience or attainment.

The experiences themselves are not so important. We crave them because of a need to validate our egos, our sense of separateness. What's important is understanding.

That sounds dry, doesn't it? True religious experience is anything but dry, and is certainly not merely intellectual.

So when we undergo a conversion experience, or any kind of religious experience, we shouldn't think we're all done. Either we've fooled ourselves, or there is greater depth we haven't yet explored. Once we stop looking, exploring, questioning, we're finished, done, literally and figuratively. We're not going to grow anymore.

Emotions can create strong impressions on us, and with singing, music, dance, chanting, rhythmic breathing, and so forth, it is often possible to drive ourselves into a frenzy or hypnotize ourselves into a blissful state of ego-absorption. Our minds become more concentrated, focused, and distracted from our fundamental nature and our problems. Sufficiently strong confusion can result in some amazing things, such as speaking in tongues. Escaping the humdrum of everyday life is a big motivator, and keeps the revival tents filled and the TV preachers well-financed. And the preachers, who depend on us for their livings, will do their best, each in his or her own way, to keep the honeymoon fever alive. Otherwise people might not keep coming back.

So while we can achieve mental stability through adopting a group and their belief system, it may occur to us at some point that our beliefs are not doing much for us, that our lives are still vague and empty of meaning. We may look inside, long and honestly, and realize that we're just biding time, fooling ourselves so we won't bolt in mindless, jabbering fear.

And life *is* scary.

Fortunately, there are far greater depths to religious experience.

8.2   Cosmic Consciousness

The next kind of religious experience I'm going to take up is in an entirely different category. It's not just head-and-shoulders above the emotion-driven experiences of the Honeymoon Effect. When you have the next variety of religious experience, you may feel very strongly that you've seen God. It's about as subtle as brass knuckles to the jaw or hot lead in the chest. Regardless of the strength of our emotional religious experiences, the experience referred to here is far more powerful. If the honeymoon effect is a ripple, this next experience is like a tidal wave. What is this religious experience?

The experience has various names, and I can't say for sure whether the names refer to the same experience, although I suspect many of them do. It has been called samadhi in ancient Sanskrit, jhana by the Buddhists, as well as kensho, or enlightenment, or seeing God, or seeing the True Self. It has also been called cosmic consciousness, or superconsciousness.

These are all words, and they are all misleading. What is this state, and how can we experience it for ourselves? While this question may be motivated by the common desire for experience and personal validation, there's no sense in not satisfying your curiosity, especially since over the centuries religious leaders have been reticent about being up front about it. That reticence is in part due to the difficulty of describing the experience in a sensible way. Those who haven't experienced it can't possibly imagine it. It is literally like trying to describe sight and sound to those blind and deaf from birth. Also, our religious leaders are often simply politicians with little or no understanding of the depths of religious experience, and might even deny such experiences out of hand, although they are clearly related in the Bible and many other religious texts.

There are many methods for inducing this state, and they all require some dedication. Concentration is key, and of course insight can make it easier, as there are two different modes of entering into so-called cosmic consciousness. I'll describe a generic method, followed by a description of the state itself.

Sit quietly in a dimly-lit room, legs crossed, back erect. Watch the air as it is passes in and out of your nostrils, and keep relaxing tensions in your body. Also relax your respiration, letting it become gentler, fainter, steadier. Do this every day, preferably twice a day, for twenty or thirty minutes each session.

Then, sometime in the next thirty or forty years, it might happen. On the other hand, it might happen tomorrow, many times, or it may never happen. It's rare, and requires a kind of persistence and natural self-discipline that few are able to muster. Diet plays a part, as does proper exercise and attitude, and keen insight certainly doesn't hurt the effort, either.

But let's go on.

As you develop deep repose and calm, it becomes natural to fall upon in-and-out breathing, so excessive force of concentration isn't really necessary. The air passing in and out of your nostrils gradually assumes gigantic proportions, because you're so relaxed and calm and there is virtually no other stimuli except an occasional thought. Even thoughts start to feel heavy and burdensome, and eventually tend to naturally fall away.

You may become aware of sheets of light, great, tranquil sheets rippling across the darkness of your being. Beginners often see spurious, rather superficial lights caused by sensory deprivation; these rippling sheets of light are different, deeper. An oval of light may form in your forehead, about where the so-called third eye is depicted. It will waver at first, then become steady, brighten, solidify and strengthen.

There are some subtle and peculiar perceptions: your eyes fuse on the oval of light, and there is something of a feeling of having only one eye, of coming into contact with the oval, becoming absorbed there. For a very brief period, there's a feeling like toothpaste going through the hole of an ethereal toothpaste tube, except that you're the paste.

Then suddenly, as in a bursting of bonds, the old world falls away. Everything in the universe, your body, your mind, your world, everything, is flooded with the most amazingly brilliant and beautiful light.

Far from some illusion or self-deception, it will strike like an iron fist, more real than anything you've ever experienced. Joy will ring through your being like a great bell as you sail without gravity or pain in an infinite ocean of pure light and bliss.

Now, some of you will probably think the above description pertains to some sort of leftover flashback or dream sequence. On the contrary: the description doesn't do it justice. Bear in mind that Jesus spoke of just such an experience: "When the eye is single, the body is filled with light." Look it up. The single eye refers to the perception that the two eyes have fused into one as they focus and become absorbed on the fuzzy patch of light that develops just prior to entrance into samadhi.

Samadhi is the experience of Moses and the burning bush, of Paul on the way to Damascus. In the Buddhist and Hindu traditions there is considerable training aimed at reaching this experience.

Similar reports are often recorded in near-death experiences, or by persons who are simply very tired and relaxed, and undergo an accidental transition into the ecstatic state. The "toothpaste tube" is probably the same as the tunnel traveled through by persons undergoing near-death experiences. Recall that there are usually reports of light at the end of the tunnel.

I have read numerous such accounts throughout my life, the most recent being that of an author in the Daytona Beach area who reported such an experience in the newspaper. He was in Vietnam, and was just lying down on his cot, dead tired, when he was flooded with light. There is nothing subtle about this experience. After it's over, though, you can't quite believe it happened. The effect on the nervous system is similarly spectacular: you'll feel wonderful for days afterward.

It's not hard to understand why, upon having such an experience, people tend to believe they've been touched by some supreme being, or seen heaven. It's so powerful that there isn't any way to forget it, or to dismiss it as insignificant. It makes a lasting impression.

A very natural question is to ask what the experience is, what it means. Some say it's God touching you. That's fairly reasonable, except for the fact that you then have to try to define God, and if you really think about it you'll find that's virtually impossible. God is truth? Sure, but where does that get us?

Another point of view is that this manifestation of energy, light, and bliss, is the "true self". There is some validity to this point of view, although it again doesn't do much for us. And there are complicated philosophies which claim that this true self is hot-wired to God, and that we're all drops in the massive ocean of bliss, which is God's body.

That description is poetic, but practically speaking, it still doesn't do that much for us. That is, it doesn't matter whether we believe these philosophies or not. It's possible to enter into this ecstatic state of consciousness even if you're an atheist. Maybe it's just our incurable habit of naming everything, intellectualizing, which compels our seeking of such inadequate and unnecessary answers.

So what is the experience and why does it exist? I don't know of any clear answer to that question. From the reports of near-death experiences and my own observations, I suspect it's connected with death, with the dropping of the body, total dissociation of the mind from the physical processes. It's suggestive of a transition to another state of being. By itself, samadhi may be taken as pure consciousness, without any physical or mental hindrances of any kind. I distrust the phrase pure consciousness, however, because in another sense, pure consciousness is unavoidable, and is encountered in our everyday life.

Physically, superconsciousness is almost certainly associated with the pineal gland, a small body inside the brain behind the forehead. This gland is mysterious in that it is equipped with photoreceptors, although light can't penetrate all the intervening tissue and stimulate them. It's considered a vestigial organ, still functional in some lower vertebrates, such as frogs. It would be interesting to find out whether this region of the brain is active during samadhi.

In any event, superconsciousness is completely astonishing. No drug, no other experience can top it. There's nothing like total, complete, clean, healthy, wonderful happiness and joy, with that amazing light filling your being, filling the universe. As one sage put it, it's the kingdom of heaven within.

Yet, in and of itself, samadhi, for all its magnificence, turns out to be considerably less significant compared to true and powerful insight, which brings us to our last category of religious experience.

8.3 Insight

Over three decades passed from my initial questioning as a five-year old on the kindergarten playground before I fully appreciated the nature of insight.

The great calm and concentration of superconsciousness, and the mental strength it gives, is impressive and no doubt reasonably conducive to the development of insight, unless it becomes a distraction. But ultimately, no amount of concentration can ever compare to the least flash of true understanding. Cosmic consciousness, or samadhi, may be thought of as spiritual muscle. Insight, on the other hand, is spiritual intelligence.

You can't force something like insight. Paradoxically, the pursuit of insight can become an impediment. People will tell you to do this or that to get the insights, or they'll be extremely deluded and tell you that it's just a matter of reading the right books and agreeing with the correct philosophy. Political correctness is often mistaken for the awakening of the mind. Similarly, some vapid sensory deprivation during meditation can be mistaken for insight. The difficulty is that we don't normally experience it, and when we desire it, we can easily fool ourselves into believing we have experienced something special.

True insight is shocking and powerful. It comes from direct perception, and like lightning striking, you see and understand in a flash. Insight is transforming. After it happens, you grasp the world in a fundamentally different way. It affects everything instantly. Strangely enough, however, insight doesn't solve all your problems. It doesn't make you perfectly happy. And unless, possibly, it's very deep insight, your new vision will come and go.

Insight, and the enlightenment it conveys, is like a door into another world. It's a world that is indistinguishable from the world we live in. It's a world that changes when we change, that refuses to change when we want it to change, a world that is what it is just as we are what we are. It's the spiritual world that all seek and few find, the world a few religious people may or may not have pointed out, a world which was promptly forgotten by their followers who, unable to break free of their conditioning, became politicians of faith.

Where and what is this world?

It's the world before our eyes.

Now, it's natural to think that just can't be so. All our lives we've heard about the next world, one better than this one, and now I'm telling you that the spiritual life is the all-too-ordinary life you already have, waiting to be uncovered. That's simply unbelievable.

Now ask yourself why it's so hard to believe.

Is it because the world you live in is so burdensome that you want to escape to never-never land? Is it because you are so bent on avoiding the humdrum, pain, and tedium of everyday life that all you can think about is where the exit is, the way out, the ticket to Disney World? Is it because you really wanted exotic experiences, something that would make you feel special, different, blessed?

We've all heard stories about heaven, hell, purgatory, and other places, astral planes, and we would like to visit them, know more about them. Our lives are unsatisfactory, and we want something different, something more.

I'm not going to tell you to be satisfied with what you've got. There's no reason to be, and that's a dead end, anyway. It's just that when we look for exotic experiences it is generally for one of several reasons: (1) We want to escape from reality; (2) We want to increase the strength of our sense of self, ego, which means we must be unhappy with what we are, and therefore we are trying to escape from reality (see 1); (3) We lust for new and different experiences, especially pleasant ones, because the ones we've got are getting worn out (see 1).

Note that all three reasons are really different shades of the desire to escape the world, to escape what we are. This attitude, this activity of escape makes it impossible for us to understand our nature. And that understanding is essential for insight, for freedom.

It's like playing tennis. The coach is always telling us to watch the ball. Instead, most of us are thinking about how we're going to whack that little fuzzy piece of rubber and knock our opponent's socks off. That distracts us so much that too often hit the ball long or into the net.

The real point of the game of tennis isn't winning. The point is hitting the ball.

In our daily life it's easy to lose sight of that. Everything is winning and losing. Television, newspapers, our friends and relatives, even our kids lay that trip on us, and we bite it off, believe in it without question.

Meanwhile, what is really important is not whether you win or lose, but how you play the game.

Now, getting back to our thesis, we're still wrestling with that unlikely notion that our miserable everyday life is somehow the spiritual world we were seeking all along. How is that possible? And if that is truly the case, haven't we arrived? Aren't we already there? Why should we try to meditate, or do yoga, or do anything at all? Shouldn't we be perfectly happy?

The answer is no, we shouldn't be perfectly happy. Why should we be? First of all, while the spiritual world is indistinguishable from the one we're living in, for most of us reading this essay that is only an idea planted by me, the author, in our collective head. We don't really see it. We have only an intellectual appreciation, at best, like the one people have when they know that smoking is bad for their health and then smoke anyway. Didn't they read the label on the package? The surgeon general has determined smoking is bad for your health. Yet they continue smoking because they haven't seen the danger with their nerves, their heart, so it doesn't make an impression on them. Intellectually, they understand, but on the gut level it hasn't hit them yet.

Recently it was shown that vision is a function of not just the eye and visual cortex, but also of the higher brain functions in the cerebral cortex. There's a feedback loop that helps fill in the gaps in perception. Many of us have had the experience of glancing at the headlines and seeing something like "CLUB RAISES MONKEY". We do a double take, and only then realize that "monkey" was actually "money". But for that instant, we clearly saw the wrong word. That's a function of the higher brain centers, filling in perceptions when information is thought to be incomplete.

In the same way, we tend to allow the higher brain to fill in a lot of other details for us. We get used to seeing the same old things and tune them out. Instead, our higher brain simply checks our situation briefly, recognizes that similar events are happening, and then returns to automatic pilot, ignoring the influx of new perceptions. We remember the way to work, for example, and don't really see the road. Later, we are surprised to have arrived safely, because we remember nothing of what happened along the way.

That automatic mode of operation is absolutely essential for efficient functioning in the world, but like any bad habit, it's not necessarily healthy. The past, as stored in our memory, takes command, and we lose our flexibility, our sensitivity, our ability to heal and grow. Nothing is fresh. We look at a stand of trees, and instead of seeing their intrinsic beauty and grandeur, we might say something like "so what, how many trees do you need?" We aren't seeing the tree; we look at it only long enough for the higher brain to cut in and take command, putting a filter of memory over the scene.

Breaking this grip of the past allows an immediate and direct perception of the spiritual world. The break occurs when we become sensitive to our thoughts and feelings, to the grip itself.

For the past, and its grip on us, is also part of the spiritual world, part of what we are.

Every day, when we awaken in the morning, we come into consciousness. We are conscious of the feelings in our bodies, our thoughts, our discomforts and needs. We're conscious of the bed covers on our bed, of a warm body beside us softly breathing, of the sound of birds outside the window, perhaps of the antics of the mind that create the geometry of our world, continually estimating the distances between the different fragments of experience. Getting up, we go to the bathroom, then to our study for quiet meditation.

All throughout this, consciousness has been happening. When we sit and meditate formally, relaxing our respiration, relaxing any tensions we may see in the body, consciousness is still happening. And regardless of what occurs during our quiet sitting, whether we daydream, or sit in restless discomfort, or perhaps are engulfed in blinding light, consciousness is still happening.

We give special meaning to the blinding light, because it seems so much more wonderful than our mundane everyday activities. It appears logical and forced that this must be so. Yet our everyday experience is not happening out there, separate from us, nor is it happening in here, in our brains, separate from the outside. It is happening in consciousness, our consciousness, so it's our world, but just as we control our bodies only very superficially, there is the rest of the world, inseparable from us, which we also control only very superficially. Without consciousness, for all practical purposes the world isn't there, and to say otherwise is an exercise of the intellect, not the simple fact of the matter.

Dividing up the world into the mundane, secular world and the transcendent, spiritual world is an exercise of the intellect, the trade-goods of the professional religious people. They've got to have something to sell, and they can't sell you what you've already got.

At this point, however, we're not interested in buying an illusion. We want the real thing: just what we are.

We have divided the world up into two pieces: self and other, spiritual and mundane. That's our world view, the one thrust upon us, and everything we do only reinforces that view. It seems like a fact of life, an indisputable law of nature.

Elsewhere I have described the alternate view, the new world view. Again, that view can be understood intellectually, which is only of slight value, because it will not really change your life. And, the depth to which this insight is grasped determines the extent to which your life is changed.

That may seem rather dry compared to the possibility of samadhi. But when you see, with your heart and nerves, with your whole being, that there is no division between self and other, that the world can be directly viewed as a single organism, together with all its beauty and ugliness, perfections and imperfections, when by some amazing grace that happens, ordinary perception is transformed.

You will see the light on the water of the river, the shimmering ripples and patterns, infinite in subtle complexity, you'll see the clouds and birds and trees and power lines and telephone poles and you will perceive them with such intensity and clarity that you will feel no separation, they will seem close, extraordinarily close, part of what you are. As you drive down the road, the roar of the car's engine, the air conditioning, the clamor of traffic will be the most engrossing and intricately beautiful music. When you get out of your car and walk, other beings will be mobile, independently acting parts of your body, just as your heart and stomach and bowels and lungs all act independently. You will feel an intensity of love which is strong and powerful and calm and firm, but which paradoxically is not soft or sentimental or emotional or instinctive.

You'll see that there is nothing beyond the horizon but your imagination, that the past and future are both functions of memory and its projections.

You'll see that everything you experience, your person, your personality, is all part of a vast being, and this being was before your eyes, and behind your eyes, inside and outside your skin, forever and always.

That's the real you. That's the real world.

Chapter 9

Meditation and Transcendence

After reading the previous chapter on the varieties of religious experience, it's natural to ask what can be done to realize such states of being. We could be coy and assert that we're already there, but the real answer is meditation. A great deal has been written on meditation and how, when, and where do it. Many otherwise intelligent and well-informed readers may feel less than competent when it comes to actual practice. Fortunately, meditation is a natural process that anyone can do. Mastery, however, is an entirely different question.

The underlying motivation for meditative practice is important, because with the right motivation we will carry on with the practice even when it appears we aren't getting anywhere for an extended period. Most of us want to be happy, and that's the fundamental, healthy motivation for practicing meditation. We'd like to become a better person, live a happier, more fulfilling life. That helps you and everyone else who interacts with you. Some people may have more complex goals, such as achieving a certain religious experience. But as a matter of fact, it's unlikely much will happen that's very dramatic. For most people transcendent states of consciousness are rare experiences. If they occur at all, they can be separated by years or decades.

On the other hand, you may be a person who sees that life, as we're led to live it, can be pretty miserable, because whatever we have will eventually be taken away from us. Maybe you see that although you feel pretty good right now, your happiness is built on sand. Maybe you are filled with curiosity, you want to find out, understand who and what you are. Maybe you're willing to invest about a half hour of your time every day, sitting uncomfortably on the floor or in a chair.

If you are such a person, then it may be that formal meditation will interest you. Some technique is in order, here, because although meditation is natural, our conditioning has trained us out of it. Formal meditation is a practice designed to help us return to what we already are, to our natural state. That natural state is transcendence. We transcend our conditioning and become what we are.

9.1   Preparations for Formal Meditation

The first thing to do is choose a good time to meditate. Best is early in the morning before anyone else is awake. Another good time is late at night, although fatigue can be a hindrance. I personally like the late afternoon outside somewhere, surrounded by nature. Another favorite time is four o'clock in the morning after a few hours of sleep.

The next step is to find a quiet place that is reasonably uncluttered in your home, or go for a walk and find a secluded tree. It's best not to meditate soon after a meal because then blood runs to your stomach at the expense of your brain, which reduces the possibility of mental clarity.

Before formal practice, it's good to stretch for a few minutes, particularly the back muscles. Make sure your back muscles are stretched out by doing alternate leg pulls or plow postures. Flexing the spine, as in a cobra pose, is also beneficial, as is a head stand, if you can safely manage one. If not, stand on your head but keep your feet on the ground, which is a good substitute. The reason for these exercises is to ensure you will be able to sit comfortably for some time. Very often, tension or other discomfort in the back will magnify during meditative practice, so the exercises benefiting the back are especially important. Increasing blood supply to the head is advantageous from a point of view of increasing alertness and focus. Formal meditation is a physical challenge.

After the warm up exercises, sit comfortably cross-legged on the ground. It's okay to use some pillows or other props if you have trouble sitting comfortably, and even a chair can be used. Hold your back erect, and take a couple deep breaths. Flex your spine and then settle into your posture. You are now ready for the practice of meditation.

9.2   Meditation Technique

There are numerous meditative techniques. In a sense, they all work. They are all simple to explain and very hard to actually implement, because as soon as you start you'll find that your mind is spinning webs of thought, your body is telling you to move, and all of a sudden there are plenty of other things you think you should be doing. That's normal. Among the techniques are methods of dealing with such impulses.

9.2.1   Mindfulness of Breathing

The most fundamental meditative practice, and the most valuable, is simple mindfulness of breathing. For most people, the nose tip is the natural place to let attention settle. As you breathe in, watch the sensation of the air passing into your nostrils, and then watch it pass out. Repeat, and continue for about twenty minutes. In the beginning it's a good idea to set some kind of alarm, because otherwise the meditative session tends to be very short, so the alarm acts to discipline you.

As you watch the sensation of your breath passing in and out of your nostrils, you should be aware of what's happening in your body. You should relax any tensions you may perceive. There are tensions around your face and scalp, and as you are aware of them, consciously relax them, all while maintaining your posture with straight back. Keeping the back straight without strain or discomfort does require some practice. Also, you should relax your respiration. What that means is that as you breathe in and out, watching your breath, endeavor to slow your breathing very gently, relax the process, so you breathe more faintly over some time. Of course you aren't physically depriving yourself by holding your breath. Just allow breathing to subside a little in a natural way.

Now, you will notice that your attention may immediately wander. You'll think about what you have to do later, or what you did earlier, or what you would like to do. The sensory deprivation may even cause your mind to conjure up images. For those not used to the practice, that's why mindfulness of breathing is a good choice, because it tends to be very calming, it composes the mind. At no time is it necessary to force your thoughts and distractions out of your mind. Just notice them and relax them away, always returning to the sensation of air flowing in and out of your nostrils.

For those who can't breathe through the nose, an alternate practice is to watch the rise and fall of your abdomen as you breathe. When you breathe in there is a slight sensation of your abdomen swelling, and you watch that sensation. Watch it when it subsides.

What is the point of this practice? What does it do? First, by sitting quietly you become aware of the typical inner chaos of your thoughts and feelings. That's a very big insight. Most of our lives we take our internal life for granted and are not aware of how we grasp after thoughts and feelings, how strongly, in every waking minute, we pursue sensory stimulation. When it is gently denied for even a couple minutes, we become aware of our intrinsic restlessness, our inability to be still and at peace.

Another benefit is that we are getting training in patience. Most situations in daily life require a certain amount of patience. Meditation practice increases our capacity for patience, facilitating every aspect of our life.

The most important insight is what most of us experience when watching the sensation in our nose. We view that sensation as being detached from us, from who we are. It seems that the sensation is two or three centimeters displaced from what we identify as our self. In fact, that sensation is part of what we are. Intellectually we can perhaps appreciate that fact, but in meditation we can see right away that we have divided the world into self and not-self. Even our own breath seems to be separated from what we are! That's a fundamental division, and in mindfulness of breathing we are watching that division in action. That's what we have to understand. When that artificial separation stops, then we find out who we are. Unfortunately, being intellectually aware is not going to transform our perception, nor will it return us to our natural state of being. It's useful, however, to realize that through the meditative technique, the situation has been reduced to simplest terms. That's one of the purposes of formal practice. Perceiving without division can be called transcendence, which is a very cool word, but not really a good description. Nondual perception does not involve going beyond what you are, but returning to what you already are.

There are a number of variations on the breathing practice and one or another might be useful for you. One variation involves counting breaths to ten, then starting over. You'll find it challenging to count them all the way to ten without becoming distracted. You might also try saying to yourself mentally "in" when you breathe in, and "out" when you breathe out, to reinforce and remind yourself what you're supposed to be doing. Yet another variation is to do nothing at all except relax. You find that when you are strong in your posture and very deeply relaxed and calm, you will fall naturally into awareness of breathing. That's a very excellent method, but it may require some considerable practice before it works for you.

Early in the practice of meditation it's common to see lights, colors, or experience a variety of sensations. Those feelings and perceptions are usually simple consequences of sensory deprivation. You may identify certain tensions as significant because you have not seen them before, but you should just relax them. If you are looking for progress of some kind, be ready for disappointment. True spiritual experience has nothing to do with weak flashes of light and vague sensations of any kind. True spiritual awakening, experiences like samadhi or insight, are extremely powerful. And while emotions can sometimes be evoked which feel powerful, spiritual experience is far more compelling. It's shocking and total, thrilling in a way you have never experienced. Transformation of consciousness isn't subtle. It's a rare experience, so you should settle in for a lengthy wait.

9.2.2   Expected Outcomes

Over time, the practitioner can anticipate some improvement in the ability to sit and relax and focus. It's common, however, to reach a plateau and remain there for years at a time and not make any significant improvement. Nonetheless, it's best to persevere. Those practicing this meditation have been shown to experience further physical development of the brain even after adulthood. The benefit of a daily retreat into calm, a period in which the mind can relax and settle, is of value in itself. The goal is not to achieve something, because you already have it. It's more a rediscovering of what you are. Even if you arrive at some sudden flash of understanding, you might not even realize it until much later.

Other possible outcomes include the development of access concentration. This is a highly advanced state where the mind is well focused and composed on the in and out breathing. At this stage a bright spot might appear on the internal vision in the area between the eyes. If it coalesces into a disk, then you are on the verge of entering samadhi, which is meditative absorption. As discussed previously, those experiencing such a state often relate that they have seen God. It's a state of high energy and extreme mental clarity, and of light and bliss. The light, unlike the vague and fuzzy flashes of beginner's practice, is truly amazing, suffusing your entire being.

The most interesting outcome is the possibility of nondual perception. That's our natural state of consciousness, and it's both very ordinary and very awesome at the same time. With mindfulness of breathing, you become aware of your dual consciousness right away, because you see your in and out breathing, the sensation near the end of your nose, and you identify it as not being attached to you, as separate, when in fact it is evident that sensation is part of what you are. Remember that the goal is not to achieve non-dual perception, because that seeking is already a function of our dualistic worldview. The goal is simply to observe what is, observe the dual perception, nothing more. The desire to reach for something else, to experience something else, is understandable, but is part of the process that led to the assumption of dualistic consciousness to begin with. Through mindfulness of breathing, we relax and calm the mind and body and simplify consciousness, and during that process there is an opportunity for non-dual consciousness to reemerge.

9.2.3 Reflections

An alternate form of meditation involves reflections of various kinds. The purpose of a reflection is to supplant negative thinking with positive thinking, and consequently to develop habits of mind that are conducive to better a better and happier relationship with yourself and with others. We have plenty of negative influences in our lives, and rather than struggle with or reject such influences, it is better to supplant them with disciplined positive thinking. This practice in turn can facilitate the development of deep calm and insight.

There are a number of negative mental states, such as envy, hatred, anger, lust, laziness, lassitude, fear, doubt, and mental restlessness. These mental states can be alleviated through insight; the problem being that we may have to wait some considerable time for freeing insights to occur. Further, such reactive states can interfere with our state of being, robbing us of the calm attention, the alertness we require in order to arrive at liberating insight. Reflections can therefore be used to reduce the power of negative habits of thought by replacing them with good habits.

Meditation on Love

Perhaps the most useful reflections are those that have the theme of love. There is no more positive thought, word, or action than that which is motivated by love. Ideally, love is spontaneous, but practicing a simulation, so to speak, can simplify and enhance our lives and therefore lead to the spontaneous expressions and experiences.

Preparations for a reflection on love follow the same general guidelines as given above. Instead of watching our breath, however, we begin to repeat a positive thought, over and over. First, because many of us have been criticized and hurt by our normal life struggles, it's important to start with positive regard for ourselves. For most of us, we are our own worst enemy, so in the beginning we focus on ourselves. Only after we feel very good about ourselves do we share the feelings with others.

What phrase you repeat is individual. You might say "May I be happy." That's very simple: just wish yourself happiness, over and over. Do it quietly, in your mind, in a leisurely way, for about twenty minutes. The phrase is not a mantra. Feel the meaning of the words deep within you as you become progressively more composed. The words are reminders for a general state of positive feelings towards others; the idea is to arouse this general state and strengthen it.

The initial benefit comes fairly quickly: you start to feel happy, just a general good feeling about yourself. There is nothing magical about that. The conscious mind is supplemented and controlled to a great extent by the unconscious mind. By repeating positive thoughts, you affect both the conscious and unconscious. The conscious mind starts to feel good because at last someone cares about it. This positive feeling is then communicated to the unconscious mind, which is in command of numerous physical responses and resources. It has been scientifically proven that a positive attitude directly impacts human health, so the benefits of this kind of refection are immediate.

Other possible phrases include "May I be free from anger and disease, may no harm come to me, may I take good care of myself, always." The reflection can be very short or it can be longer, more elaborate. Attitude is important: you don't want to demand happiness, only offer best wishes. Demands are stressful and counterproductive. The wrong attitude can rapidly reduce the benefits of this reflection.

Now, after you feel very composed and happy, you can turn the reflection to some other person, say Jack. "May Jack be happy, may no harm come to him, may he be in good health." Usually you choose someone you already like but are not interested in romantically. It will work regardless, but you could find yourself dealing with physiological reactions. That isn't a disaster, but could be distracting.

Another way to practice this meditation is to reflect "May all beings, in all directions, be free from sorrow and despair, may they be happy, free of health problems of all kinds." You can direct this kind feeling to every quarter, south, then north, east and west, then up down, in all directions, imagining all the beings in a given direction and wishing them well.

There are numerous related reflections, such as a compassion reflection, sympathetic joy reflection, and equanimity. The reflections you develop are again personal and simply repeated during a relaxing formal meditation. Again, you can start with yourself: "May I be free of suffering, may my health and well-being improve each and every day." These thoughts can be extended to particular other people, or to everyone: "All beings suffer, may they be free from their suffering, may their health and well-bring improve each and every day," is a general compassion reflection.

Sympathetic joy is the capacity to experience the happiness of others as your own happiness. In the hippy jargon of old, this might be called "a contact high". Someone else is happy, and it makes you happy. Sympathetic joy may be considered the antithesis of envy, where the success and happiness of another makes you gloomy, wishing you could be like that fortunate other person, and have what that person has. The success of others is truly your own success, because success makes the world a better place, regardless who achieves it. Again, a personalized formulation can be devised for meditation encouraging this mental state. "May my good fortune and happiness continue and increase." The reflection is not a mantra, but a reminder. As before, after a few minutes of wishing this state on yourself, you can wish it on some close friend, and eventually include everyone. It's similar to the generic meditation on love or compassion.

Equanimity is a poorly understood word that many confuse with an unfeeling, uncaring state. Rather, equanimity is the cultivation of highly alert state of mental readiness, unswayed by the throes of emotional tumult and confusion during events that would otherwise be upsetting. That freedom from the roller coaster of emotion permits you to act in situations calling for it, or to be calm when everyone else is flustered and upset. When you are calm in such circumstances, it helps others achieve a similar calm, and deal with the inevitable problems and frustrations of life without making them worse by reacting to them. A reflection might be: "May I be calm and collected in all circumstances. May I face the trials and tribulations, failures and successes, with a steady mind and heart, with alertness and even temper." The reflection can again be extended to others after a suitable period of practice. As before, the words are not the point, here; they are reminders. In thinking the words, we endeavor to sense that state of mind and heart within us and amplify its strength. This strength can be wished on others.

Other Reflections

Other reflections can amplify other desired, positive qualities. A simple one I use spontaneously and often is: "I can and I shall." It's an empowering reflection, and we all need more of that feeling because we have a lot of good deeds on our agenda, and many of them require some considerable effort, and time is short. Reflections can even enhance will power during dieting. Think to yourself, "May I be free of excessive desire for food; may I prefer healthy meals of fruits and vegetables". To gain energy for any endeavor, it is also beneficial to reflect on the transience of phenomena and of our own existence. That kind of reflection can engender a quiet sense of alertness and energy. You become more aware that you are literally running out of time.

At the end of the day, whatever you want to arouse in yourself can be enhanced by the way you think and what you think. A few minutes of investment every day in disciplined, directed positive thinking can have an excellent general effect, because ordinarily we allow our minds to flit and wander in an aimless way. Any practice that temporarily focuses our thoughts in a positive way will have a lasting influence throughout the day.

9.2.4   Meditation in Action

Meditation is not limited to sitting cross-legged on the floor. There is no rule that says we have to retreat from our normal daily activities. Meditation can happen any time, and in any place. Unlike formal practice, which focuses on particular subtle activities or feelings, meditation in action takes anything and everything as the source of inspiration. During most of our waking hours we are engaged in dualistic perception, so any and every thought, feeling, or sensory experience is fair game for the practice of meditation. We literally can't miss; training opportunities arise constantly everywhere.

9.2.5   General Advisories on Formal Meditation

Some may feel inadequate when it comes to meditation and express a need for someone of greater experience to provide guidance. The techniques presented here, however, are so simple and innocuous that you don't need anyone. Further, many of the those claiming to offer guidance are just as confused as you are, so you might not be any better off than before. You can do it by yourself.

Another concern many people have is that meditative practices violate some personal religious belief. I think that all religions have advocated some form of meditation, and most of them recognize the value of calming and purifying the mind, so there's not much point in worrying about that. Whoever the ruling deity of the universe may be, he or she will be happy you're doing something about your mental clutter.

The physical requirements of formal meditation may also create barriers. It's uncomfortable to sit still for even a few minutes. The solution is to experiment with different postures and props and discover what works for you. It's best to keep it simple. Part of the practice is finding a way to remain comfortable and still for extended periods. In the beginning, ten or fifteen minutes is fine. An hour is a considerable challenge for most people, and is probably a good target the first year of practice. Once or twice a day for about twenty minutes is a good regimen, with a single longer session once a week. Like anything else, with practice you improve.

9.3   Miscellaneous Observations on Meditative Practice

If you observe thoughts and feelings carefully, you may often find that such subtle experiences seem to be hanging nearby in space. You feel innately that the thoughts and feelings are separate from what you are. Of course, they aren't: they're part of what you are. It's therefore of interest to pay attention to them, to notice that perception of division. That can be extended to so-called external objects. In our usual dualistic mode of perception, a nearby bush or distant cloud appears incontrovertibly separate, outside of us, not part of what we are. Again, such perceptions are an opportunity to see just what we're doing.

True meditation is very simple. You sit, you relax, you watch. What do you watch? It doesn't make a whole lot of difference. Just watch whatever is happening. The sensation of the breath going in and out of your nose tip is a good choice, because it's happening all the time. It's also calming, and deep calm clarifies the mind, predisposing it to insight.

Now, as you observe, what happens? If you're like most people, your mind wanders away into compulsive thinking almost immediately. You will notice that thinking about things, such as your girl friend, what you are going to do when you arise from your posture, or a myriad of other thoughts, creates a subtle background of feeling and sensation that is basically pleasurable. It's a sense of self that we all take for granted, but which is really just a mode of escaping the feeling of emptiness that otherwise yawns before us. Formal meditation becomes little more than thirty minutes of self-distraction, absorption into automatic thinking that is pleasurable and rather pointless, except for that general background buzz it gives you.

The reaction to this inevitable distraction is usually that it's bad and must be stopped by force. Naturally that is not the case, and the use of excessive self discipline is more of the same problem, the past dictating how you should be and what you should think and feel. Rather, noticing the ease with which we become distracted is an important insight. Watch it, catch yourself in the act. The distraction then becomes meditation in action.

So the goal is to just keep on watching, observing phenomena as they arise, observing the gap, the division you have created. Because, just as your feelings of depression are not truly separate, neither is anything else.

Now, what's happening when you sit and relax like this? Why should it be so helpful? Again, the answer is amazingly straightforward. Daily life can take on a very complicated appearance. Our minds, through their conditioning, have become similarly complex. The stimuli and our reactions to them are coming so fast and furiously, and our minds are so wild and out of control that it's difficult to see what's going on.

Natural, deep relaxation simplifies perception enormously. You're awake, but you're just sitting there and there isn't much happening. It becomes possible to begin noticing some of the basic facts of life, facts about your mental processes, gaining important elemental insights.

What kind of insights? For example, many people don't realize just how dependent they are on stimulation. They find it very difficult to sit still even for a few minutes. Their minds work in furious overdrive, trying to keep up the level of distraction, something they've never noticed. It's also possible to work out feelings during meditation, because the active passivity allows them to play themselves out and lose some of their power over us.

Prayer has many similar benefits. Prayers generally last only a few minutes, but have a calming effect on the mind. Positive reflections such as previously developed will have similar effect, but are more powerful than prayer, which often is poorly focused.

Most people will go through their entire lives and never experience more than a peaceful sensation from meditation. Of course, that's quite valuable, and well worth the small investment. Others will gain insights, and perhaps get very composed. At this point, meditation can be fun and exciting, because you never know what might happen when you sit down and start relaxing. How calm can you get? Well, you can get so calm that your breath is just barely going in and out, and the whole universe seems to be contained in just that sensation of your breath going into and out of your nostrils, which, practically speaking, it is. That depth of composure is very fine. Pleasure is not the word. Descriptions that come to mind are strength, fearlessness, purity, and powerful calm.

With very hard, long practice, some may experience samadhi, as described in the previous chapter. The existence of such a state can hardly be disputed, because it has been observed by many of those having near-death experiences, and of course many sages throughout history.

I am personally acquainted with an emergency physician in Jacksonville who directly observed someone returning from a near death experience. He related that once he had a patient die on the table. The patient, in his early fifties, had been having chest pains. He called his doctor, who got him a prescription of nitroglycerin, but a few hours later the pain was still increasing, so the man called an ambulance, which took him to the hospital.

Enter my friend, the ER physician. The victim was on the table, and his heart went into ventricular fibrillation. The doctor grabbed the paddles and gave him a jolt of voltage. The man's body leaped and arched, but his heart stopped. The doctor gave him another slap with the paddles. The man's heart started back up, and he regained consciousness. His first words were: "Wow! That was something else!"

He went on to describe that he saw himself lying on the table, as if he were floating above his own body. He then passed into a tunnel. There was beautiful music, and a brilliant light at the end of the tunnel.

I don't know for a fact whether the light seen in near-death experiences is the same light seen during the transcendent experience known as samadhi, or jhana to the Buddhists, or maybe satori to the zen priests of Japan. It seems likely, however, that there is a close connection between those reported states of consciousness. There is some variation on this experience; you may feel suspended in the midst of an endless blue space, bright with light, or filled with brilliant gushers of light, like a fountain.

Now a caveat: I have met people who experienced rather ordinary neural flashes, born of sensory deprivation and the like, and mistook them for some kind of enlightenment. Most of the time you can tell if this is the case by looking at the person when they describe it. Usually the description is rather vague. They might even say it was subtle.

The true experience, however, is about as subtle as an iron gauntlet exploding under your chin.

Many people are reluctant to reveal details of this experience. It's a risk, because then you might have other people "faking it", fooling themselves, and then trying to fool still others that they've had some great experience. Also, expectations tend to rise, so it's easier to get frustrated, especially when you can count on years to a lifetime before you break through.

Another good reason to keep it under wraps is that most people are not going to believe you. Even if they believe you, they haven't experienced it themselves, and so they can't grasp what it is you're talking about, anyway. And you could experience a general loss of credibility that could be damaging to your career.

As I've mentioned a number of times, it really doesn't matter what anybody thinks. They will, or they will not, find out the truth for themselves. Belief doesn't enter into it.

At this point you may have developed some idea that meditation is something you must do cross-legged. There is nothing further from the truth. The fact of the matter is, you can meditate while eating, drinking, walking, making love, driving, or playing cards. Most of the time, however, we're too busy daydreaming, and thinking, semi-consciously spinning yarns to ourselves, to ever meditate, and when we do something it's a matter of coercion, where we force our minds onto a particular object, like breath. The very activity of coercion means we are still operating as if there is a division between the internal and external worlds.

Try as you might, getting rid of this "me-ness" is virtually impossible. Fortunately, that isn't a problem. After all, it's a valid part of your experience–it's part of what you are. A lot of the time I just hang out watching myself cut things in two. Just keep your eye on it, or on whatever else comes up into your focus. Watch those pleasure-producing daydreams. They're interesting: they're part of what you are.

Do we need to think about what we're observing, like a scientist? No. Insight, as discussed here, is through direct perception. In fact, it's even possible to develop some strong insight and not be aware of it, as such.

The experience of samadhi, the great light, is impressive, but as far as religious experiences go, it's not in the same league of true insight. Practicing simple relaxation as I've outlined in this essay will predispose the mind toward insight and true enlightenment, which involves understanding the nature of consciousness, with how we immediately grasp the world. That sounds dry compared to seeing God, so you'll have to take it on faith that it isn't.

Other practical matters that must be addressed, in regards meditation, are things like diet, exercise, livelihood, and family life. Naturally, eating well and not too much is important to the meditative life, as is exercise, which keeps the circulation in good shape. If you eat too much, blood gets shunted from the brain to the stomach, reducing mental acuity. Having a job that doesn't totally exhaust and beat you down is important, too, if you can manage it. Finally, a stable family life is a big plus. It's hard to get these various technical, mundane details in order, to reduce confusion and maximize your mental sharpness, but ultimately it's all part of your training, and training is important.

Let me summarize my personal recommendations.

(1) Maximize Your Life Situation Get your life in order, as much as possible. Improve your diet, simplify your relationships, get your work routine straightened out.

(2) Set Daily Minimum Goals Set a certain realistic daily minimum target for the formal practice of yoga exercises and meditation. I suggest half an hour a day, to start with, seven days a week. When you do something positive every day, it eventually starts to have a cumulative impact on you.

(3) Practice Mindfulness As you move about your daily activities, watch what's going on. It doesn't matter what you observe, just whatever your attention naturally falls upon. Don't analyze, just observe with your nerves.

(4) Simplify Meditation Practice Make your meditation simple. Sit with a straight back and relax any tensions you may see. When you get extremely calm, the mind falls naturally onto in and out breathing, anyway. Remember that you are not trying to achieve anything special. You're just seeing what's there, what you already are.

(5) Be Yourself In some sense we are all falling short of our expectations. We can all improve. However, that's the past speaking, our memories and our projections, our expectations, which are also the product of our confusion. And we don't want to get rid of our confusion; that's what we're most interested in, because that's what we are. So we don't need to try to be someone special, we need only be what we are.

(6) Nurture Independence Go on your own. Spiritual leaders can be either helpful or not. The point is, you couldn't possibly know if they are being helpful, coming from the confused state you're in. Remember that these so-called advanced beings wear pants or skirts just like you do. Looking to someone else for guidance can too often be used as an excuse for putting off doing something yourself.

Remember: You are the oracle. You are the discovery waiting to happen.

Chapter 10

Practical Spiritual Living

Through most of this book I have discussed the nature of consciousness, love, and religious experience without much reference to any particular practices. Practice may even seem superfluous, because we have often discussed how goal-oriented thinking and perception can be a significant barrier to developing insight.

Our mental environment, however, can be significantly enhanced by certain practices. If insight comes from mental clarity, it's evidently advantageous to maximize the probability that we think clearly. So in this chapter I will make various recommendations for those readers interested to getting such advice. There are several categories of activities to get in order. The aim is optimizing mental clarity, and all the common sense advice, and then some, must be applied in order to achieve this goal.

10.1 Diet

The body is a machine. It requires fuel, and oxidizer to burn the fuel to make energy. The first and foremost requirement, therefore, is to put the right kind of fuel inside the tank.

Most of us eat what we like, or whatever we can afford. In more affluent countries, where food is abundant and people can afford to buy it, people generally eat too much. It's important to eat quality food in the right amount.

What kind of food should be eaten? Food should be relatively light, easy on the digestive system, and nutritious. A diet rich in vegetables and fruit is best, with some grains. Rice and vegetables, for example, digest fairly quickly. Within an hour or so of a meal, the body feels light again. Heavy meats should be avoided, although fish is fine. A strict vegetarian diet will usually result in some slight amino acid deficiency, so it's convenient to have some source of animal protein as an occasional supplement. Many people are sensitive to the fact that animals are aware, capable of suffering, and wish to avoid meat of all kinds. Milk and cheese products, which are produced without any slaughter, might be substituted for meat in those cases. There are also certain beans, such as soy beans, that are loaded with useful protein.

Quantity of food is also an important parameter. Those who eat mainly fruit and vegetables don't have to worry: they can eat as much as they want. Everyone else has to be a little careful. While it isn't illegal or immoral to be overweight, it is definitely a detriment to mental clarity. The extra pounds must be carried around, and in addition it sometimes makes it harder to exercise. When food goes into the stomach, blood is shunted away from the other parts of the body and directed to the stomach. That's why we feel drowsy sometimes after a big meal. With lower blood flow to the brain, there is a natural loss of mental acuity. So the quantity of food ingested must be limited. Food is best taken in the morning or midday. There is a saying which addresses this: "Eat breakfast like a king, lunch like a prince, and dinner like a pauper". Most of us have to get up and go to work in the morning, so we need a good meal at the start of the day. At the end of the day we're just winding down and going to sleep, so it isn't necessary to have a large meal. Further, at the end of the day, we may find a little free time to ourselves for meditative practice, and a light stomach will help in terms of mental clarity.

10.2   Relationships

The way we relate to people profoundly affects our spiritual well-being and our ability to carry on with our quest for understanding. There are a few guidelines that may help us steer a course through the many complications of everyday relationships.

Keep your relationships simple. Try not to load too many expectations on those you relate to, and expect the same treatment in return. Very often those around you will indulge in complex mind games, because of their insecurities or because they want to squeeze something more out of you. There is no reason to take this personally: most people are so self-interested that they aren't even aware when they're treating you unfairly, or using or abusing you. You're living in a confused world full of confused people, and you yourself may be confused. Don't make it more complicated than it is by taking things personally.

Similar advice can be of value in sexual relationships. Even under the best of circumstances, sex can really complicate our lives, which is why parents always worry about the sex lives of their maturing children. If you're dating, the most important aspect is honest communication. That's a catch-22, because it's always possible that neither party knows how to communicate, or one person communicates and the other refuses or is only faking it. That's normal; people are always on their best behavior around others they don't know well. They sometimes hide their real self until much later, sometimes years later. If, early on, the person seems difficult, don't spend too much time trying to figure it out. They're being difficult because they have a number of unresolved issues. If you have made a good effort to communicate and compromise with the other party and she or he is still being unreasonable, then try not to worry about it any more. Some people can't be pleased: it's in their genes, or it's their conditioning. Do your thing, and let the significant other go do his or her thing. There are plenty of fish in the sea.

I realize clear thinking in romantic or sexual relationships is much easier said than done, and have plenty of experience dealing inadequately with such problems. Our emotional chemicals are taking us for a ride. That's another reason why it's important to work to develop insight, because in fact with strong insight, you can free yourself from the tendency to fall into romantic obsession, albeit usually much too late to do you any good. One consolation: if you don't make the right decisions and end up with a difficult, demanding, and unreasonable mate, you will at least have the benefit of considerable spiritual training, just in tolerating the situation.

Regardless, it's important to remember that both you and your partner are imperfect. It's normal not to agree on everything, and to see things in your partner that you don't like. You don't need to take every problem to heart. Try to address problems early in the relationship and be vigilant. Problems that are evident to you and to any other reasonable person might be opaque to the very person causing the difficulty. It is possible to fall into relationships that have persistent, unresolved problems. You could say two such people are incompatible, which is a general true statement that conveys very little real information. Unfortunately, you sometimes find yourself between a rock and a hard place, and must just make the best of things. A good sense of humor is a must.

Similar advice applies to the workplace. If you are in a good work environment, then you have nothing to worry about. Bosses, however, often become bosses because they want to have control and push other people around. They will often have a complicated view on how things should be done and how you should conduct yourself. It's important not to take them personally when they criticize you unjustly or micromanage you, which in the case of a bad boss will happen quite often. Maintain your sense of humor, try not to take it personally.

As far as our own conduct, we should strive to be independent, self-supporting, and industrious. Never ask someone else to do something for you if you can reasonably do it yourself. That's common courtesy. It's also important to recognize when others are using you for a door mat, and take corrective action. The motive isn't really justice, or even your own well-being, it's in everyone's best interest.

Finally, relating to your children, if by chance or grace you have any, will give you some of your very best training. A child is a miracle and a terrific trainer. We can learn a great deal from them.

My parting advice on relationships is: good luck, you'll need it!

10.3 Daily Meditation

Understanding meditation and how to use it is fairly important, because it is one of the primary tools for calming the mind and opening the door to the possibility of insight. We have discussed some technique and some insights concerning meditation in previous chapters, and here we'll take it up again, but from a more pragmatic point of view.

True meditation is rare. What most of us are doing, most of the time, is a simulation. In true meditation, we let go of the past and experience an immediacy and intensity of perception that is nothing short of miraculous. Most of us, however, are confused or unhappy because we haven't ever been able to let go. Letting go, here, doesn't mean just giving up on life. It means arresting the use of the past, of memory, to adjust or color our immediate, everyday perceptions. When we do this, powerful meditation is taking place.

As previously stated, however, it's hard to let this happen. So in the beginning it's a good idea to develop some formal meditation practice.

The most basic method of meditation is mindfulness of breath. This practice involves sitting quietly in a room and watching the breath go in and out of the body. The nose tip is best, the most tranquilizing, and in today's go-go world, we need the strongest medicine. This type of meditation is conducive to insight, because most people, after getting in practice, will very clearly perceive a distance between what they call themselves and the sensation of the air going in and out of the nose tip. This is the fundamental division that we have created in our world. Evidently, the sensations in our nose tip, of the air rushing in and out, are part of what we are, but we observe them and have the feeling the sensations are separate from us. It isn't necessary or desirable to react to this realization, or try to suppress the perception. That's simply the problem trying to imitate a solution. Continue to watch the sensation of the breath going in and out.

It's normal to wander away in some fantasy or habitual thought while doing this kind of exercise. That's not a big deal. You'll find that you're always wanting to think of something, and it's mostly to escape the reality of what you're experiencing, which is not very thrilling. When you notice your mind wandering, take a deep breath and gently settle back on the nose tip. Alternately, simply relax more deeply. When deeply enough relaxed and calm, thoughts begin to seem very heavy, and it may happen that you'll drop them effortlessly at some point.

As previously stated, there are a number of reflections that can gently persuade the mind to give up some of its self-defeating reactive behavior. Hatred, lust, and foggy, deluded habitual thinking are all impediments to deeper insight. These can be softened by the right kind of reflections.

In a previous chapter, we looked at how quietly wishing happiness to yourself and also to others, over and over, can calm the turbulence of anger and lead to an opening of the heart. Again, the technique is simple. Sit quietly and repeat 'may I be happy' over and over. Imagine taking care of yourself, being kind to yourself. As you get adept at this practice, you will find that even a few minutes of this reflection can significantly improve your mood. My son, as a boy of ten, will actually start to laugh with even a moment's practice of this reflection. After you feel happy, extend the wish to others, gradually widening the sphere of influence to include everyone and everything. Similar reflections can focus on developing compassion, and the ability to experience joy at the accomplishments and happiness of others. Finally, this same sort of reflection can create states of deep equanimity. Powerful equanimity may not seem to be a desirable state, but it isn't passive, it's powerful. As negative events assail you, the ability to remain unperturbed can maximize all outcomes for everyone.

Lust is a normal everyday occurrence for most people. This includes lust for material possessions as well as sexual lust. It even includes lust for states of superconsciousness or insight. A good reflection to reduce lust is to make an inventory of your body parts. Again while sitting quietly, review all your parts, imagining them one by one, over and over. This has the effect of creating an objective view of something which is taken very personally. Lust can also be much more subtle; a grasping after the subtle sensations created by habitual thinking. It's important not to use suppressive techniques. Watch and learn, these phenomena are part of what you are.

Reflections of various other kinds can be helpful. Reflecting on the impermanence of phenomena, and the transitoriness of life, can increase the motivation for spiritual practice. Impermanence is a fundamental quality of life, and while most people think of this in terms of old age and death, it's better understood as a moment-to-moment phenomenon. Sensations arise and fade, experience is in continual flux, continuous change. Nothing is the same the second time.

In developing your formal meditation practice, it's important not to try for too much, nor expect too much. As previously stated, not much happens most of the time, nor is it supposed to happen. Relaxation is what you're primarily going to get on a daily basis, a peaceful feeling. You'll feel better grounded. A little bit every day is more important than a lot of meditation on rare occasions. It is also a good idea to have more than one session every day: one or two short sessions of a few minutes, then a longer session of half an hour or so.

Relaxation is a discipline. As you sit, look for tensions in your body, and whenever you find them, relax them. You'll find that it's hard to relax when you've eaten too much, or eaten the wrong kind of food, or slept too much, or not exercised properly. The mind can't see clearly, nor the body relax, if basic health has been neglected.

Meditation has been called a quest, but it's more of an adventure. In a quest, we have a goal or we seek an answer, but an adventure is its own answer. We are a world, and discovering what we are is the greatest adventure.

10.4   Physical Conditioning

A lot of what has been discussed here may sound abstract and intellectual, but in fact it isn't. It has to do with clarity of perception, relaxation, and calmness. Keeping the body healthy and fit is therefore very important. What kinds of exercise are best?

Most exercise is beneficial. Weightlifting is one of the few exceptions, unless the weights are fairly light. The best exercise increases stamina, respiratory capacity, flexibility, and circulation.

The very best form of exercise to accomplish all this is yoga. There are many different kinds of yoga, but the kind referred to here is Hatha Yoga, which is the yoga of physical exercise. This kind of yoga involves systematic stretching of all the muscles in the body, a strengthening of the spine, and various respiratory exercises. Any bookstore or library will carry books on yoga, and the best books have plenty of large, easy to follow photographs. It's not generally necessary to read a lot of directions, just assume the positions shown in the photographs. It's not really critical to do the exercises exactly right, because there are numerous variations on any given pose, and it's likely you're doing one of those variations by accident.

It's important to remember that the model will likely be extremely limber and hard to imitate. Never try to force a stretch. A good rule of thumb is that the stretch should be comparable to the good-morning stretch everyone takes when first getting up in the morning. It is very possible to injure muscles or tendons by overzealous stretching, and by holding the postures too long. In the beginning, do the exercises two or three times each, but hold them only ten seconds or so each time. Later, at the end of some months of experience, the poses can be held for a minute or two or longer, slowly relaxing into the posture, never applying excessive force. Body weight alone can be used to good effect.

The hardest aspect of yoga is the discipline of daily practice. In general, yoga should be practiced six times a week for about an hour each time. After some experience, up to three hours can be safely practiced, although this much yoga is rather extreme. Most people don't have that much free time. A shorter session of daily practice is more important than less frequency but longer period of practice. When you practice regularly, you can really tell the difference. It's easier to relax into the stretches and get a thorough workout.

Yoga gently stretches the muscles, relieving tension, liberating energy. Many people have hidden tensions, especially in the back, often caused by stress. Yoga relaxes those tensions through stretching.

Other forms of exercise that are particularly valuable include walking and swimming. Running is highly aerobic, but hard on the joints, and middle aged and older people can easily injure themselves. A good, brisk walk is better. Disciplined swimming, distances of around five hundred meters and more, can relax and rejuvenate the body. The combination of swimming and yoga is especially excellent.

For those who are extremely out of shape, or who have special medical conditions or injuries, it's advisable to proceed slowly after consultation with a physician. It can be very difficult getting the energy and discipline for daily exercise, but it's important to remember that even a very small amount will help. Decide on some minimal exercise commitment, say five minutes, that you will do every day without fail. You'll find yourself exceeding that time frequently. The hardest part is simply developing the daily habit.

10.5   Yoga: A Primer

In this section a basic yoga workout will be described that is suitable for a beginner. These are among the first exercises I learned forty years ago, and I still practice them today.

10.5.1   Introduction

The practice of yoga has as its primary goal the optimization of the health of the practitioner. Working through the body, yoga also helps to improve the environment of the nervous system and mind. A distant goal is the realization called *samadhi*.

Beginners should develop a set of about twenty exercises that they do every day. The exercises should be done three times each, but held only for about ten seconds each repetition. Altogether, the session will last between a half hour and forty minutes. The daily practice is extremely important: one day a week can be missed, but more than one day greatly reduces the benefit.

After about six months, the exercises can be done twice for about a thirty seconds each repetition. By the end of the year, and sooner if the practitioner feels ready, the poses can be done once for a minute or two each. When in good form, some exercises can be held much longer, and there is benefit in doing so: the head stand, the shoulder stand, the bow pose, the leg pull, and the alternate leg pull are in this category. In fact, as you age, it usually takes longer to get the muscles to soften and relax. They have to be trained over months of time, and then the training must be maintained or they go back to their previous state. Some, like the alternate leg pull, I hold five minutes or more, because it does a great job of stretching out the lower back muscles. I have done twenty minute head stands, a fantastic physical stimulus. In general, however, it's best to progress slowly, because especially in the beginning muscles and ligaments can be overstretched and injured, even if you feel fine at the end of a session. You will feel the pain the next day!

One common error is for a practitioner with an injured muscle or ligament to decide to "stretch through" the pain. Athletes often train while in pain. Such training while injured is very inadvisable. In cases of mild strain it may be possible to train while some slight sensitivity is still apparent, but in general there is a significant risk of making the injury worse. It's best to forego those postures that affect the injured part of your body until you have thoroughly healed, and then recommence very gently and work slowly back into form.

It's best to start with standing exercises, which tend to be a little easier to perform, and then to progress to the floor postures. Postures need not be executed perfectly. At first, approximations to the correct pose are usually necessary. The repetitions can be done one after the other, or the whole set can be done three times. While holding a posture, time can be measured by counting breaths. In this way it's possible to adjust the length of time the workout requires. As you learn more postures, you can count the number of postures you do, as well. If I have a busy day and run short of time for yoga, I might do between forty and fifty exercises and hold them for five to seven breaths each. In general, I like to do one hundred poses, counting between ten and twenty breaths for each, and sometimes double that for the head stand, alternate leg pull, or plow, and similar exercises. That's a very fine work out, which will make you feel like you're walking in the clouds. For more exercises, consult any number of excellent books devoted to yoga.

The pranayama, or breathing exercises, are generally done only once, at the end or in a separate session. Deep breathing during the postures is important; the motion of the lungs expanding and contracting helps with the stretching. Above all, listen to your body.

10.5.2   Physical Goals of Yoga

The goals of yoga can be broken down into some fairly large categories. Most important is the stretching out of the back muscles. A great deal of tension is stored there, and that tension can cause fatigue and irritability. So in yoga there are many exercises in which the body is bent forward, which stretches out those all-important back muscles: the cow posture, the leg pull, alternate leg pull, and triangle poses are examples. Those exercises also stretch the hamstrings and other leg muscles, improving circulation to the extremities.

Another important area is spinal alignment and flexibility. Our spines are composed of disks, and it's important for them to be aligned and for the spine to retain some flexibility. In these poses, the back is arched, which causes the spinal disks to align properly with each other and which also improves spinal flexibility. Examples include the cobra and bow poses, chest expansion, and the dancer pose. Spinal flexibility is also increased by the twist pose, among others.

The next important area is balance. The dancer and tree poses help improve and maintain balance, as does the standing pose. The ability to balance decreases with age, so those exercises are especially important for older practitioners.

Finally, yoga works on respiration. There are of course a number of pranayama exercises such as the complete breath or the bellows breath. Those exercises improve the oxygenation of the blood and the general health of the lungs. They generally also help produce a state of calm. Deep breathing while holding the poses also benefits respiration.

When yoga is done regularly for about an hour and a half a day, seven days a week, the body makes great strides in improving circulation and respiration. The immune system becomes highly responsive, so the practitioner rarely gets ill. When in good yoga shape, the muscles cooperate readily and you experience a healthy glow in them as you stretch. Nerves are calmed by elevated levels of certain neurotransmitters, such as GABA, or gamma-aminobutyric acid, which has been proven to increase due to regular yoga practice. Yoga is one form of exercise that can be practiced all our lives. It makes for a very comfortable, healthy and flexible body, which in turn promotes a comfortable, healthy, and flexible mind. Through the stretching exercises of yoga, anyone can improve their physical and mental well-being with half an hour or so of practice a day, and doing up to two or three hours a day is even better!

In the next section I present a beginning set of exercises. As you advance in your practice, you will want to do many, many more. I do up to one hundred forty different exercises in a single session.

10.5.3 A Set of Elementary Exercises

1. Standing pose: Stand straight up, pulling the belly in, straightening the spine, standing at attention. Take a deep breath, raising the arms and locking the fingers overhead, palms upward. The practitioner can also rise on the balls of the feet at the same time, if desired. Hold for ten seconds, exhale. The exercise is good for balance and posture.

2. Cow pose: Standing with feet shoulder length apart, take a deep breath and raise the arms along the body, stretching them overhead. Exhale and bend forward slowly, dangling at the waist. After about ten seconds or so, slowly stack up the vertebrae, keeping the chin tucked in on the chest, returning finally to a standing position. This exercises stretches hamstrings and back muscles, and promotes circulation to the brain. It's very relaxing.

3. Chest Expansion: Stand with feet shoulder length apart. Lock fingers together behind your back at the small of your back, like you're praying behind your back. Take a big breath, arch backwards for about three seconds, while trying to pull your hands over your head. (Don't hold too long–you may pass out!) Bend forward, still pressing up with your arms and hands, exhaling in the process. Slowly rise to standing straight again. The exercise flexes the spine and stretches the chest muscles, all while enhancing circulation and oxygenation.

4. Triangle Pose: Put the right foot forward, left foot at a forty-five degree angle. Bend and place the right hand on the right leg, or beside the right foot, left hand straight up in the air. Repeat with left foot forward, right foot at a forty-five degree angle, and left hand by the left foot. This is a great exercise for stretching lower back muscles and the hamstrings, and in addition benefits balance.

5. Reverse Triangle Pose: With the right foot forward, left foot at a forty-five degree angle, rotate and place the left hand on the right leg, or beside the right foot, with the right hand in the air. This exercise is harder than the regular Triangle, and puts a twist into the torso, as well.

6. Dancer's Pose: Standing with feet shoulder length apart, lift the left foot and reach behind the back and take hold of it with the left hand, arching the spine and raising the right arm. Repeat on the other side. A balancing pose, the exercises also flexes the back and stretches the quadriceps in the front of the leg.

7. Tree Pose: Shift the weight to the right foot and place the left heel comfortably against the right inner thigh. Put the palms together and slowly raise them overhead. It's a very gentle balance pose that also gently stretches some leg muscles and promotes the ability to focus and concentrate.

8. Stomach Rolling: Stand bent slightly over with the chin up and hands on your knees, feet about shoulder length apart. Press all the air out of your lungs and then expand your rib cage, isolating the abdominal recti. Bunch the stomach muscles in and out a few times, and then try rolling them back and forth. This takes a little practice. Exhale and repeat several times, massaging internal organs.

9. Cobra Pose: Lie on your stomach. Placing the hands under your shoulders, push your chest and shoulders up, arching your spine, raising your chin. The hips can stay on the floor or lift up. This exercise is great for spinal flexibility and in addition stretches and expands the chest.

10. Locust Pose: Lie on your stomach. Put your fists under your hips to create a fulcrum. Raise both legs using the muscles in the small of your back. Hold. This is a difficult exercise that strengthens the all-important lower back muscles.

11. Bow Pose: Lie on your stomach. Bend the knees and reach back, grasping your feet. Usually, this means holding onto the tops of the feet. Arch you back and turn your body into a bow, lifting the head and chin and the legs, with arms under tension. The Bow Pose is a great physical stimulant, a good one to hold for twenty breaths, if that can be manages. It improves spinal flexibility, general arm strength, and increases circulation to the vital organs.

12. Knee and Thigh Stretch: Sit with the soles of the feet touching. Hold your feet in clasped hands and pull upwards, leaning back a bit. The exercises stretches out the knees and groin muscles, helping the practitioner develop a more comfortable cross-legged sitting posture.

13. Leg Pull: Sit with legs straight out in front. Take a deep breath, raising the arms. Exhale and arch forward and grasp the legs, or toes, wherever it gives a comfortable stretch. Hold and breathe normally. The exercise benefits hamstring and other leg muscles, shoulders, and back.

14. Alternate Leg Pull: Place the heel of the left foot close in to the crotch. Stretch the right foot out. Do a leg pull on the right leg. Repeat on the opposite side. This is a great back-stretcher with a slight twist, of course also benefiting the hamstrings. In general, it should be held longer than many of the other exercises.

15. Shoulder Stand: Lie on your back. Raise both legs and try to straighten your body, supporting your back with your hands, elbows on the ground. The mother of yoga exercises, shoulder stands convey numerous benefits.

16. Plow Posture: Lie on your back. Raise both legs and try to place your toes on the ground behind your head. The Plow Posture stretches out the back and neck muscles, among many other benefits.

17. Half-spinal twist: Sitting, put the right foot on the floor outside the left knee. Wrap the left arm around the right knee and twist to the right, stretching the right arm to the right around the body. Repeat on the other side. Aside from twisting the spine and improving its flexibility, the twist stretches various muscles in the legs and buttocks and neck.

18. Yoga mudra: Sitting cross-legged, or in half lotus, or full lotus, whichever is comfortable, clasp the hands behind the back and lean forward. Then slowly raise the clasped hands as far up as possible. This exercises improves the cross-legged sitting postures.

19. Child Pose: Kneel on the mat and bend forward, placing your head as close to the ground as possible with hands clasped because your back. With fingers locked, the arms can then be raised, if desired, as if you are trying to lift them over your head. The Child Pose stretches out the knees, shoulders, and back muscles.

20. Head Stand: Kneeling on the floor, clasp hands and make a triangle with hands and elbows. Place the head in the hands with the crown on the floor and thumbs helping support the head. Stand up with feet on the floor. This is sufficient for a start, and some practitioners who are uncomfortable with the full head stand stop here and hold. In the absence of an assistant, the full exercise can be practiced next to a wall. In that case try to kick the feet up in the air and get your heels to rest against the wall. Be careful to support your head and neck. Push slightly off from the wall and try to balance. In the beginning, it's really best to have someone assist you, if possible, when doing the full pose. When performing the head stand away from any support, there is a danger of falling over backwards. If this happens, you should keep your fingers loosely laced and in position on the floor so as to protect your neck, and go into a forward somersault. The head stand is often called the father of yoga exercises. The exercise stimulates and tones the entire circulatory system as adjustments are made to handle the inversion of the body.

21. Complete Breath: Sitting cross-legged, in half-lotus, or full lotus, press all your air out of your lungs, then take a complete breath, filling the abdomen, then the chest, then gently lifting the shoulders. Hold briefly. Exhale. Repeat seven-ten times.

22. Bellows Breath: Sitting cross-legged or on the knees, take three rapid complete breaths. The fourth breath, hold the breath and lock the chin down on your chest. Hold for several seconds but not to discomfort. Exhale and raise the chin. Repeat a total of three times. The bellows breath is highly stimulating. It's probably best not to do it too many times in succession.

23. Alternate Nostril Breathing: Sit cross-legged with back erect. Put the index and middle finger of the right hand on your forehead. The left nostril can then be closed with the ring finger and the right nostril with the thumb. Take a complete breath through the right nostril, and exhale through the left. Inhale through the left, and exhale through the right. That completes one round. Do seven to ten rounds. The exercise focuses the mind on the air passing in and out of the nostrils and promotes calm.

Chapter 11

On Driving Down Clyde Morris

In this essay I'll be taking a more personal point of view. In it, I'm going to describe in detail the event that resulted in my writing this book. Most of what I have expressed in these pages came to me during a few seconds of time while I sat behind the wheel of my old Volvo, driving down Clyde Morris Boulevard.

For those of you into motorcycles or car racing, you might know that Clyde Morris is a major artery connecting Ormond with Daytona Beach. Daytona, of course, is Mecca for the auto-racing set. At any rate, the event I'm about to describe had a tremendous impact on me. In an instant I understood more than I ever got out of a thousand books like this one.

One of the biggest problems facing spiritually-minded people is how to integrate their spiritual practice with everyday life. Most of us have to spend a lot of time making a living and dealing with our primary relationships, and the older we get, the more things seem to encroach on our free time. There is a tendency to put off our practice in favor of what appear to be more pressing needs. The kids are clamoring, our mate is nagging, our bosses are bossing. There's always someone or something standing in the way, and there's a tendency to think that, someday, those distractions will magically disappear and we'll be able to get on with the business of understanding what we are.

Here's the reality: it's very unlikely the so-called distractions will just get up and go away. And if they do, others will rush in to fill the void.

Sure, there's always retirement. We can do our thing while collecting our social insecurity. The problem with that idea is our failing health and faculties, brought on by age and especially by letting ourselves go while riding life's big merry-go-round. Unfortunately, procrastination isn't going to cut it. We've got to do something and do it now.

But to put it all in a personal perspective, I'm going to scroll back in time to the seventies.

Many years ago, when I lived in a garage apartment and took the bus, walked, or rode my bike everywhere, a few odd jobs were sufficient to keep me living like a king. There was plenty of time for reflection and a daily exercise regimen, which included about an hour of yoga. When it became clear to me that being a lifeguard and swimming instructor simply wasn't going to cut it as a career, I embarked on a course which ultimately resulted in my becoming a scientist and educator.

The demands of science, particularly physics, are considerable. As a student, I regularly put in sixty to eighty hour work weeks, combining classes, study, and research with supporting myself as a teaching assistant. Looking back, I'm amazed I could ever have made myself do it. It changed me. I started out as a Florida Cornflake, and voluntarily jumped head first into Physics Nerd. It got to the point where I thought a tough fifty-page calculation was a good time. I regularly passed up nights out on the town with family and friends in favor of perusing pages and pages of mathematical hieroglyphics.

In any event, I found myself skimping on my daily practice of yoga and formal meditation. While I never gave it up completely, I frequently missed days, fell out of shape often, then got only halfway back into shape, over and over again. At the time it seemed that the weekly demands in my chosen career took precedence over everything else. I figured that when I got out of school it would get easier, and when it got easier, I'd get back into my regimen.

Well, I was half right. After graduate school life got a little easier, and I had more time on my hands. But then came the birth of my daughter, an amazing, high-maintenance kid whose mission in life from day one was to help me experience the boot camp I missed out on. My former life was shattered, utterly destroyed by a few pounds of upchucking, demanding, wailing wonderfulness. Time seemed to be in shorter supply than ever. It finally began to dawn on me that I needed to make some changes.

The first plan I implemented was to keep track of the number of hours I put into my practice on a daily basis, requiring of myself a daily minimum investment of time. I had done something similar in school when taking certain demanding courses, which in physics is all of them. For my spiritual practice, I budgeted a minimum of one hour a day. This hour comprised both yoga and meditation. If I did only half an hour, then I would drop to "one half hour down". If I did three hours in a day, then there would be a surplus of two hours which I could use to eliminate part of my deficit. Whenever I got back to zero, I'd be caught up.

Later I started jotting down a record of my daily activity, which seemed to work better. It's important to realize that rigid maintenance of the schedule isn't important. Just keeping track helps increase the awareness of the activity, making it more likely something will happen every day. In this way I got back into a fairly regular routine, although it was still a little choppy. The problem, I realized only later, was that my commitment was built on an intellectual foundation.

That brings us to the next and most important part of the story.

The success of the organizational tool I'd developed was encouraging, but certain questions still remained. It had been years since I'd had the leisure to go on meditation retreats, and as I approached forty years of age it began to look like I never would again. Twenty years had gone by in a flash and, due to a special kind of relativity, the next twenty were going to go faster still. Not only that, but I was getting a little middle age spread! Pretty soon I'd face less than optimal health, old age and disease. So I felt I had to do something, not just for my own sake, but for others, for my children. I felt strongly that I needed to make a better effort. Except in the very beginning, I'd always practiced alone, which meant I wasn't really working with anyone or helping anyone. I was beginning to feel that I was shirking my responsibility to society.

Getting away from a spouse and kids for a few weeks of meditation is very difficult, especially when they don't share your enthusiasm for monotony. Further, you have parental responsibilities which must be attended to. Like many people, I'd always thought that real progress in meditation was out of reach without retreating from the distractions of everyday life, that somehow insight was a function of hours spent cross-legged beneath trees. With a few exceptions, the books you read and the people you talk to encourage that point of view.

In reality, however, nothing could be further from the truth. The truth is that daily life provides far greater spiritual challenges than the life of a monk or nun, cloistered in retreat.

The secret, which took me over twenty years to discover, is the understanding of mindfulness.

Meditation, for many, is a process in which sensory input is minimized. The meditators go to quiet places, sit down and close their eyes, and begin doing whatever they think is going to open the door–repeat mantras, watch the breath, reflect on God, recite holy scriptures, or gaze at internal images. This is a process of concentration, and has the advantage of calming the mind down. It's even possible, through such practices, to have ecstatic experiences, such as the Buddhist jhanas, Hindu samadhi, or possibly the Zen satori.

The problem with such practices, however, is that they require time and special circumstances. Both of those are in short supply to a person with work and family responsibilities.

Mindfulness, on the other hand, is of a different nature. Mindfulness can be practiced all day long, during any activity. Rather than having a particular object, it takes any object whatsoever.

Many activities, such as doing the dishes or playing with a two-year old, are very repetitive and sometimes tedious–perfect opportunities for the practice of mindfulness! Think about it: You can either watch your breath go in and out for an hour, or make a doll do the same dance over and over again to delight your daughter. What's the difference? Both are repetitive, both can be tedious!

It may be I don't appreciate playing dolls as much as some people do. For my daughter and I it was a daily activity, and except on those occasions when I fell into mindfulness, it did sometimes become somewhat tedious.

Regardless, given the difficulty of finding time for intensive practice, I decided that I would have to develop mindfulness, which is meditation in action, because I realized that otherwise I might never have an opportunity to deeply explore the nature of consciousness.

Yet there were tremendous barriers to implementing this plan.

First of all, anybody who can keep their mind on anything for five minutes is, in my view, a very amazing person. Some people think they're doing it, but they're just not noticing the spurious activity. Others brutally force their minds to cooperate, and get good at cracking the whip, which is a kind of spiritual fascism. As simple as the idea of mindfulness is, it's still extremely difficult to put into practice.

Let me give you an example. I might be driving, and practicing the awareness of my breath while doing so, or watching the movement of my hands on the wheel, or sometimes even watching the road. Within seconds after commencing this practice I may start to notice some unpleasant or bothersome sensations. To escape those sensations, like gas roiling through my gut or simply a poignant memory, my mind would typically drift into daydreams or random thinking.

Now, when I talk about unpleasant, I don't mean the feelings are like hair shirts or beds of nails. Believe it or not, there are a lot of things that happen moment to moment in our bodies and minds that are annoying, things that we've learned to tune out. Boredom, for example, is a common affliction, and most people don't care for it. Sometimes, after an hour of dolls, I started to long for that hair shirt or bed of nails! At any rate, there are subtle and not-so-subtle unpleasant experiences occurring quite frequently in our daily lives.

And to escape those tiny, moment-to-moment unpleasantries, we often turn to thought.

The reason for that is simple. Thinking creates sensations, and just as music can drown out unwanted background noise, thinking can drown out momentary discomforts by laying down a covering of rather bland sensation. It's preferable to think about something and feel a marginally pleasurable sensation than observe what we really are. When thought alone can't do it, we sometimes look for stronger medicine, like TV, or beer and pizza.

Thinking, associated with subtle muscular tensions, is to a large extent what gives a person a sense of separate individuality. There is nothing wrong with thinking in itself, and it's certainly a necessity, but like alcohol or other drugs, or sex, or jogging, it can be used as an escape.

As a theoretical physicist I've spent a lot of time engrossed in deep thought. It's great fun, a great escape, for me to sit down at my desk and spend a few hours putting mathematical hieroglyphics to paper. I enjoy it to this day.

Getting back to our story, the bottom line is that while mindfulness, meditation in action, was a great idea in theory, I spent years trying to put it into practice with at best limited success. Whenever I tried to focus on the minute-by-minute events going on around me, I soon found myself overwhelmed by the tedious details. Spinning away into random thinking seemed unavoidable.

What was I doing wrong? I couldn't figure it out. I even began to think that maybe retreating periodically from society was the only answer after all. Or that my stubborn do-it-yourself attitude was getting in the way.

Then one day I was driving to work down Clyde Morris, that great boulevard connecting Ormond Beach with Daytona, on my way to work. My boss had been giving me some mixed signals, telling me he was going to lay me off due to shortfalls in enrollment, then raising the hope of continued employment whenever there was a particularly challenging job he needed someone to do. I was thinking some about that, wondering if I was going to be laid off, contemplating new career moves.

As usual, however, almost as an afterthought, I was observing events, feelings, the unrolling of the road before me, the trees and the telephone poles. And in my peripheral vision, I saw my body sitting in the seat, arms up, hands on the wheel. Thoughts and various other sensations were bubbling away. Business as usual.

My first realization that something different was going on was my perception of the big, white fluffy clouds floating well beyond me, above the road and trees on either side. The clouds seemed supernaturally close, intimately close and clear, just like my breath and the occasional bubbles of thought.

Suddenly the world transformed. Everything was alive, vivid and vibrant, full of energy. The clouds floated through my body. The trees at the side of the road and the cars racing by were fragments of my being. All perceptions, both internal and external, I experienced as parts of a single whole: consciousness was everywhere, and that consciousness was the beginning and the end of all things. Everything was sharp and clear and compelling, everything was ordinary and at the same time breathtakingly beautiful. I felt positively giddy with energy, as if I were skydiving, and I laughed. That direct perception of a world without division was Truth, Beauty, and Love. It was shocking and impossible, a stunning and unbelievable vista.

When I arrived at the university a few minutes later, I resolved to write everything down. I was still amazed and incredulous, but I had seen it with my own eyes: the world and I, whole, complete, a single entity. The universe was a single being, and all those parts I called me, myself, and I were only parts of that whole. The universe begins and ends in the intricate veins of a maple leaf, ineffably beautiful. Telephone poles by the road are a marvel of imperfect order, and the roaring, rumbling motorcycle revving beside you is wonderful music. The limping vagrant is as inspiring of awe as a fabulously conditioned athlete jogging by, both of them essential and inevitable parts of the whole. In that state of natural, wholistic perception, ripples on the water go rippling through your body. You perceive the myriad leaves on a tree all at once, individually and collectively.

The experience is sufficiently astonishing that I could blame no one for not believing it.

I found that in that same moment much else became clear, particularly with regard to the practice of mindfulness and meditation. I always had the idea that being mindful meant I had to direct my mind to pay attention to certain exterior or interior phenomena. Essentially, I was dividing the world up into two pieces, me and everything else. That simple process takes a lot of energy. Further, I was picking and choosing my objects of attention. It hit me like a brick that mindfulness is far easier when you realize that what you focus your attention on has no intrinsic importance whatsoever. You can watch your breath go in or out, or observe a woman walking down the street. The object is unimportant. In every case you are observing consciousness, which is what you want to understand. That results again in a terrific savings in energy, because there is no need to use self-coercion to make yourself focus on a particular thing.

Consciousness is nothing other than what it contains. Everything you experience is part of your consciousness. Your keys, your car, your reflection in the mirror, the people walking down the road, the thoughts you think, they're all happening in the same field, one and indivisible. And far from being an abstract idea, the truth of nonduality can be perceived directly. One look transforms the understanding of what it means to be alive. It transforms your relationships. There are no adversaries, no us versus them. Nondual consciousness is love in its most absolute sense. Action that springs from it is compassion.

Many years after this event I met a student at ERAU who had a similar experience. Once again, it happened behind the wheel of a car. He was Mexican, son of wealthy and successful parents. As a teenager he got involved with gangs and drugs and became angry and resentful of his parents. He began leading a self-destructive life. At their wits' end, his parents arranged for him to be kidnapped and smuggled out of the country to a detox center in Florida. After being released from the program a few weeks later, he was driving when he underwent a similar experience of nonduality. It changed his life. He immediately mended his family relationships and began studying engineering, becoming a model student and citizen. Even a momentary glimpse of the world as it truly is–whole, complete–can have a dramatic and positive impact on a person's life.

It's possible, as we've seen in previous essays, to intellectually appreciate the reality of the nondual world view. After all, our experience is put together in our brains; when we see a tree, we are not seeing the tree itself, but rather a representation of the tree assembled in the visual cortex. Some have used this intellectual explanation to argue that only the "internal" world exists–they say that everything is happening "in your mind". But where's your mind? In your head? And it obviously isn't "your" mind, anyway, because only small fragments of the whole are under your control!

There was a time I liked to imagine there was some sort of amazing unity of everything in time and space, all the galaxies and supernovas, the atoms and molecules, all wrapped up together in some kind of grand design. Maybe there is–states such as samadhi encourage that idea. My view now, however, is that the real cosmic consciousness is the immediate consequence of the perception that the division of the world into self and other is a convenient fabrication.

Seeing the separation between observer and observed is in fact very easy. Understanding that it's unnecessary is also easy, at least intellectually. Seeing the world as an undivided whole is difficult, however, because we're always trying to see it intellectually! It's a vicious cycle.

Here, let's just do it. Sit down and watch the flow of air going in and out of your nostrils. As you settle down and focus, you may begin to become aware of that dual column of air currents as being, say, just a couple centimeters away from you. Your eyes are closed and the air is going in and out, and you can see-feel the flow just in front of you.

Of course, the flow isn't in front of you. It's a sensation you're feeling, so it *is* you. Everything you experience, good, bad, beautiful, or ugly, is what you are. Yet somehow those air columns in your nose tip still feel separate from "you". That's the separation of self and other that you have created. Easy, isn't it? You don't want to get rid of it, you just want to keep an eye on it. That's what you are: you're creating the division, and you are the division.

So after twenty years I discovered an entirely different mode of perception, completely at odds with my previous world view. I discovered that there was no need to give up the slings and arrows of daily life and retreat for twelve years in a cave. Through mindfulness, meditation is possible anywhere, by anyone, at any time. And through it, there is an enrichment of understanding that turns ordinary everyday life into something altogether extraordinary, just the way it is.

Seeking a spiritual life? Seek no further. You're already in the midst of it, along with all the problems you thought you were going to leave behind.

Chapter 12

Symphony

In the previous chapters, we've seen that there's a possibility of an alternative to the traditional world view, wherein the personality is central, occupying one side of the fence, considered interior to self, while most of the rest of experience is on the other side of the fence, considered exterior to self. In this new world view there is only a single field, not two fields separated by a fence.

We've learned that all of our books, our learning, our beliefs, are of little intrinsic value. They're band-aids, temporary relief, and we keep applying them until we look like mummies, patching ourselves up but never healing because we're afraid to look at the wounds.

We've also learned that our central problem involves the old world view, the self, the ego, that curious collection of labeled sensations and memories that dominates our lives, considered so important that even questioning it can raise eyebrows and start talk of insanity. Yet we have also learned that this limited self makes up a fair part of the whole, and hence must be loved and given its due.

There are other parts of the totality, of course, such as other people, trees, oceans, automobiles, the Sun and the Moon, microbes and stars. Those fragments enter into consciousness on a regular basis. And frequently the self-fragment has a number of duties to perform in regards the other parts of the whole. That's called working for a living.

Yet we're cut off from that unified vision of the world because of our conditioning. We've been trained to operate on the basis of thought, which is a function of memory and the past. And because of this, because of our separatist world view, repeated negative experiences can accumulate in the mind until we're boxed in, trapped in a prison of our own making.

Yet this tyranny of the past can be broken when we first glimpse the true non-duality of everyday life. Because others are not separate, we experience less anxiety in talking to them about difficult subjects, which means we don't suffer so much from being awkward or tongue-tied. The increased fluidity is catching: other people start to get along better with us, so we become more successful without having to resort to crass manipulation.

We become more generous, because giving to others is like giving to ourselves. Their happiness becomes our happiness. We leave bigger tips and are more inclined to trust people, and in turn they instinctively trust and respect us. We are also less likely to shy away from disciplining others when the occasion asks for it.

Impressing other people becomes less important. Balance is the word: machismo falls by the wayside, and we find ourselves listening to people more, even to those who are obviously wrong or out of their minds. Often those people have hidden messages for us, and some of those messages may be deep or important.

Our minds become open to the immense beauty of everyday life; the shifting patterns, the sounds, the shimmering light on the water, the pelicans diving, plunging into the sea as the foam catches the Sun and a thousand reflections play across the restless water. The intensity of everyday perception becomes amazingly strong; it's as if we've never been alive before.

All of this, a universe, can be ours. Smells, tastes, sounds, light, touches that are new and intense and fresh and clean. The past can be seen for what it is: not some heavy baggage of vague memories and emotions and guilt, weighing us down, but merely one part of the whole. Once we get acquainted with what we are, there's no ending to it. Every day is new and different, each day is the beginning and the end.

A student recently asked me if I believed in a spiritual life. I could see from her expression, from the words she used, that she was talking about souls, heaven and hell, and so-called religious experiences. I answered in the affirmative, for there is a spiritual life.

That spiritual life is our daily life. There isn't any other, and that life is discovered in the present moment, right here and now. The future is a reflection of the past, of our conditioning, just an expectation, a collection of ideas in the mind.

It's all in our point of view. We're hurting, our past experiences are weighing on us, and they're piling up to such a degree that we don't think we can go on. The future seems like more of the same, more illness, more burdens, more this, more that, always more! And what we have is inadequate, never enough.

The world is covered by a gauze of our own creation. We have created a veil and placed it over everything, a layer of memory and expectation. Nothing seems compelling anymore, nothing is beautiful; everything is drab and humdrum. We're marking time, paying our dues at the local spiritual clubs, waiting for our spiritual life to start after we check out of here and into some big mansion in the sky.

The spiritual life is now or not at all, and it is indistinguishable from our everyday life. We are the pain, the pleasure, the suffering, the sorrow, the ugliness, the beauty, the triumphs, and the disappointments! They're all part of the whole, the world that is inseparable from us, the world to which we are seamlessly joined. The past exists only in memory, and the future is just a speculation based on the past, and those are both far smaller parts of the All than we'd ever dreamed.

We are a magnificent evolving moment, an undivided whole, and that's our journey, our adventure, the uncovering of what we are. To see that requires patience; it might be a year, or a decade, or the next moment. We watch the flow of experience like stalking tigers watch their prey, keenly observing what's in and all around us, just as it is, not analyzing it or trying to get something from it. We just relax, watch, and feel. In this way, the stranglehold of the past can be broken and true healing can begin. And with the healing of the mind comes the possibility of finding the right path, of discovering what we truly are, of awakening to love and entering light.

Printed in Great Britain
by Amazon

25946127R00066